ON INFORMATION SYSTEMS

Video training courses are available on the subjects of the ... books in the James Martin ADVANCED TECHNOLOGY LIBRARY of over 300 tapes and disks, from ALI INC., 1751 West Diehl Road, Naperville, IL 60566 (tel: 312-369-3000).

Database	Telecommunications	Networks and Data Communications	Society
AN END USER'S GUIDE TO DATABASE	TELECOMMUNICATIONS AND THE COMPUTER (third edition)	PRINCIPLES OF DATA COMMUNICATION	THE COMPUTERIZED SOCIETY
PRINCIPLES OF DATABASE MANAGEMENT (second edition)	FUTURE DEVELOPMENTS IN TELECOMMUNICATIONS (third edition)	TELEPROCESSING NETWORK ORGANIZATION	TELEMATIC SOCIETY: A CHALLENGE FOR TOMORROW
COMPUTER DATABASE ORGANIZATION (third edition)	COMMUNICATIONS SATELLITE SYSTEMS	SYSTEMS ANALYSIS FOR DATA TRANSMISSION	TECHNOLOGY'S CRUCIBLE
MANAGING THE DATABASE ENVIRONMENT (second edition)	ISDN	DATA COMMUNICATION TECHNOLOGY	VIEWDATA AND THE INFORMATION SOCIETY
DATABASE ANALYSIS AND DESIGN	**Distributed Processing**	DATA COMMUNICATION DESIGN TECHNIQUES	TELEVISION AND THE COMPUTER
VSAM: ACCESS METHOD SERVICES AND PROGRAMMING TECHNIQUES	COMPUTER NETWORKS AND DISTRIBUTED PROCESSING	SNA: IBM's NETWORKING SOLUTION	THE WORLD INFORMATION ECONOMY
DB2: CONCEPTS, DESIGN, AND PROGRAMMING	DESIGN AND STRATEGY FOR DISTRIBUTED DATA PROCESSING	ISDN	**Systems In General**
IDMS/R: CONCEPTS, DESIGN, AND PROGRAMMING	**Office Automation**	LOCAL AREA NETWORKS: ARCHITECTURES AND IMPLEMENTATIONS	A BREAKTHROUGH IN MAKING COMPUTERS FRIENDLY: THE MACINTOSH COMPUTER
SQL	IBM's OFFICE AUTOMATION ARCHITECTURE	OFFICE AUTOMATION STANDARDS	SAA: IBM's SYSTEMS APPLICATION ARCHITECTURE
Security	OFFICE AUTOMATION STANDARDS	DATA COMMUNICATION STANDARDS	
SECURITY, ACCURACY, AND PRIVACY IN COMPUTER SYSTEMS		CORPORATE COMMUNICATIONS STRATEGY	
SECURITY AND PRIVACY IN COMPUTER SYSTEMS		COMPUTER NETWORKS AND DISTRIBUTED PROCESSING: SOFTWARE, TECHNIQUES, AND ARCHITECTURE	

INFORMATION ENGINEERING

Book I   Introduction

A   *James Martin*   **TRILOGY**

INFORMATION

Book I   Introduction
Book II   Planning
Book III   Design

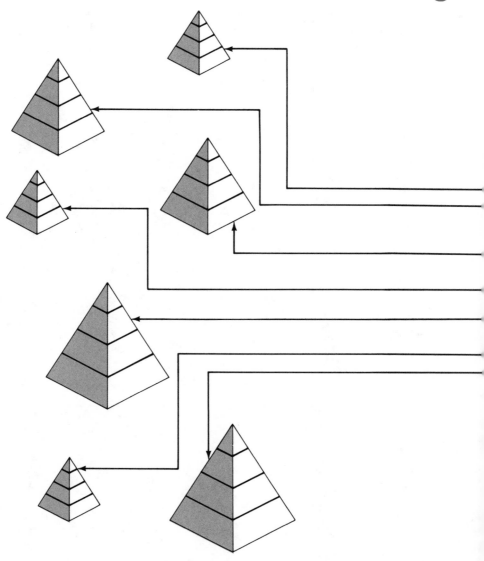

ENGINEERING

and Analysis
and Construction

JAMES MARTIN

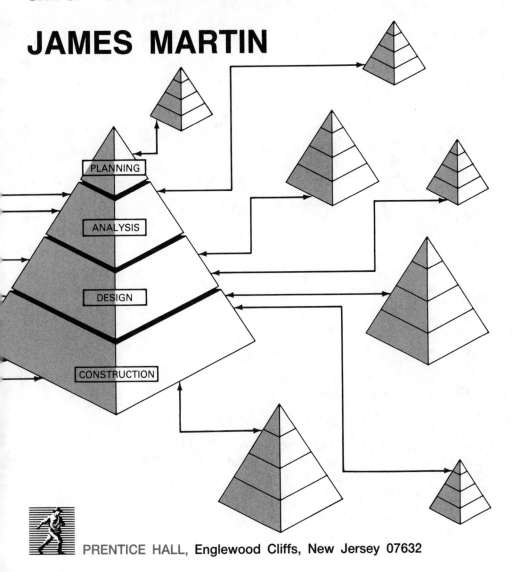

PRENTICE HALL, Englewood Cliffs, New Jersey 07632

Library of Congress Cataloging-in-Publication Data

MARTIN, JAMES. (date)
   Information engineering: a trilogy / by James Martin.
     p. cm.
   "The James Martin book."
   Includes bibliographies and index.
   Contents: v. 1. Introduction.
   ISBN 0-13-464462-X (v. 1):
   1. Electronic data processing. 2. System design. I. Title.
QA76.M3265 1989   88-39310
004—dc19   CIP

Editorial/production supervision: *Kathryn Gollin Marshak*
  and Karen Skrable Fortgang
Cover design: *Bruce Kenselaar*
Manufacturing buyer: *Mary Ann Gloriande*

Information Engineering, Book I: Introduction
by James Martin

The publisher offers discounts on this book when ordered
in bulk quantities. For more information, write or call:

  Special Sales
  Prentice-Hall, Inc.
  College Technical and Reference Division
  Englewood Cliffs, NJ 07632
  (201) 592-2498

Printed in the United States of America

10 9 8 7 6 5 4 3 2 1

ISBN   0-13-464462-X

PRENTICE-HALL INTERNATIONAL (UK) LIMITED, *London*
PRENTICE-HALL OF AUSTRALIA PTY. LIMITED, *Sydney*
PRENTICE-HALL CANADA INC., *Toronto*
PRENTICE-HALL HISPANOAMERICANA, S.A., *Mexico*
PRENTICE-HALL OF INDIA PRIVATE LIMITED, *New Delhi*
PRENTICE-HALL OF JAPAN, INC., *Tokyo*
SIMON & SCHUSTER ASIA PTE. LTD., *Singapore*
EDITORA PRENTICE-HALL DO BRASIL, LTDA., *Rio de Janeiro*

TO CORINTHIA

Information engineering is defined as:

> The application of an interlocking set of formal techniques for the planning, analysis, design and construction of information systems, applied on an enterprise-wide basis or across a major sector of an enterprise.

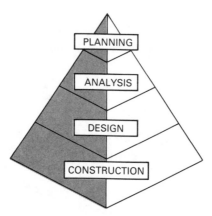

Because an enterprise is so complex, planning, analysis, design, and construction cannot be achieved on an enterprise-wide basis without automated tools. Information engineering has been defined with the reference to *automated* techniques as follows:

> An interlocking set of automated techniques in which enterprise models, data models and process models are built up in a comprehensive knowledge-base and are used to create and maintain data-processing systems.

Information engineering has sometimes been described as

> An enterprise-wide set of automated disciplines for getting the right information to the right people at the right time.

INFORMATION ENGINEERING
A trilogy by James Martin

BOOK **I** INTRODUCTION

BOOK II # PLANNING AND ANALYSIS

BOOK **III** DESIGN AND CONSTRUCTION

CONTENTS: Book I

PREFACE

I first used the term *information engineering* in courses conducted in the IBM Systems Research Institute in New York in the early 1970s. The thrust of these courses was that it was necessary to apply top-down planning, data modeling, and process modeling to an enterprise as a whole rather than to isolated projects; otherwise we could never build a fully computerized enterprise.

Since those days the techniques of information engineering have been greatly refined. Information engineering (IE) is too complex to do with manual techniques. It needs a computerized repository to accumulate and automatically coordinate the mass of detailed information. It needs tools to help in I.S. planning, data modeling, process modeling, and the translation of these models into working systems. The early tools were crude, but nevertheless provided some early experience which led to the refinement of IE techniques.

The full flowering of IE capability had to await the evolution of integrated CASE (computer-aided systems engineering) tools and the use of these tools to drive a code generator. With these tools we create a repository of planning and modeling information in an enterprise, use this as input to a system design workbench, and generate code from the system design.

The staff of James Martin Associates practiced information engineering, using computerized tools, in many corporations. They steadily refined the methodologies that are described in these three books. As with other engineering disciplines, it became clear that IE needs rigor and professionalism; the computerized tools enforce rigor and guide the professional.

Corporations that have gone from top to bottom in IE, in other words, have done the planning, built the data models and process models, and used these to design systems and generate code, have found that they can coordinate their information systems activities, build systems faster, drastically lower their maintenance costs. Once the data models and process models exist, corporations can make competitive thrusts with computerized procedures much more quickly.

The world is becoming an interlaced network of computerized corporations. As electronic data interchange among corporations grows with intercorporate networks, the windows of opportunity become shorter. We are evolving to a world of just-in-time inventory control, electronic funds transfer, corporations having their customers and retail outlets on-line, programmed trading, a computer in one organization placing orders directly with computers in other organizations, and automation of many business decisions. In such a world the corporation in which data processing is in a mess, with spaghetti code, uncoordinated data, and long application backlogs will not be able to compete. The techniques of information engineering are vital to the competitive corporation.

The future of computing is a battle with complexity. The complexity of enterprises is steadily growing. The complexity of information processing needed in the military and government is overwhelming. We can win this battle with complexity only with automated tools and automated methodologies. The challenge of every IS executive is to evolve as quickly as possible from the mess of old data processing, to the building of systems with clean engineering.

Computing needs an engineering discipline with automated tools which enforce that discipline.

James Martin

INFORMATION ENGINEERING

Book I   Introduction

1 WHAT IS INFORMATION ENGINEERING?

INTRODUCTION   *Information engineering* is defined as

> The application of an interlocking set of formal techniques for the planning, analysis, design, and construction of information systems on an enterprise-wide basis or across a major sector of the enterprise.

Software engineering applies structured techniques to one project. Information engineering applies structured techniques to the enterprise as a whole, or to a large sector of the enterprise. The techniques of information engineering encompass those of software engineering in a modified form.

Because an enterprise is so complex, planning, analysis, design, and construction cannot be achieved on an enterprise-wide basis without automated tools. Information engineering (IE) has been defined with reference to *automated* techniques as follows:

> An interlocking set of *automated* techniques in which enterprise models, data models, and process models are built up in a comprehensive knowledge base and are used to create and maintain data processing systems.

IE has sometimes been described as

> An organization-wide set of automated disciplines for getting the right information to the right people at the right time.

Just as software engineering is practiced slightly differently in different organizations, so there are variations on the theme of information engineering. IE should not be regarded as one rigid methodology, but rather, like software engineering, as a generic class of methodologies. These variants have in common the characteristics listed in Box 1.1. The methodology must be formal, computerized, and accepted throughout that part of the enterprise which practices information engineering.

In traditional data processing, separate systems were built independently. Systems were usually incompatible with one another, had incompatible data, and could be linked together only with difficulty. Some enterprises have hundreds of incompatible computer applications, all difficult and expensive to maintain. These systems are often unnecessarily redundant and expensive, and the information needed for overall management control cannot be extracted from them.

With information engineering, high-level plans and models are created, and separately built systems link into these plans and models. Particularly important are the data models of business areas. Associated with this is a model of the processes in each area. These models constitute a framework that is rep-

BOX 1.1   Characteristics of information engineering

- IE applies structured techniques on an enterprise-wide basis, or to a larger sector of an enterprise, rather than on a project-wide basis.
- IE progresses in a top-down fashion through the following stages:
  —Enterprise strategic systems planning
  —Enterprise information planning
  —Business area analysis
  —System design
  —Construction
  —Cutover
- As it progresses through these stages, IE builds a steadily evolving repository (encyclopedia) of knowledge about the enterprise, its data models, process models, and system designs.
- IE creates a framework for developing a computerized enterprise.
- Separately developed systems fit into this framework.
- Within the framework systems can be built and modified quickly using automated tools.
- The enterprise-wide approach makes it possible to achieve coordination among separately built systems, and facilitates the maximum use of reusable design and reusable code.
- IE involves end users strongly at each of the stages above.
- IE facilitates the long-term *evolution* of systems.
- IE identifies how computing can best aid the strategic goals of the enterprise.

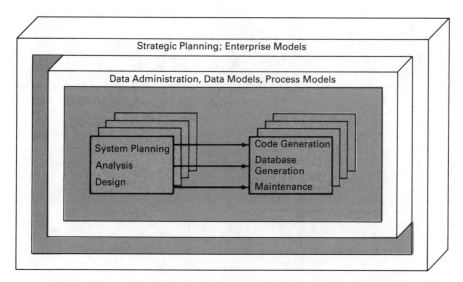

Figure 1.1 The development of individual applications is done within a framework of data modeling and process modeling, which itself relates to strategic planning of how to improve the enterprise with technology. Book II of this trilogy discusses the framework and its methodologies in detail. Book III discusses the red part of the diagram and its methodologies in detail.

resented in a computer. Separately developed systems fit into this framework. A set of automated tools is used which enable systems to be designed and constructed relatively quickly within the framework.

Figure 1.1 illustrates the framework. The outer framework relates to strategic planning. It is concerned with how technology can help the enterprise to be more competitive or meet its goals better. The framework inside this is labeled *data administration, data models,* and *process models.* Data models and process models of a business area are created independent of any specific applications in the area. Multiple computer applications will be designed and built (the inner red part of Fig. 1.1) and this will be done with computerized tools which make them fit into the framework. Different teams in different places at different times will build systems that link into the computerized framework.

THE PYRAMID   It is useful to draw a pyramid to represent corporate information systems I.S. activities (Fig. 1.2).

At the top of the pyramid is strategic planning. This needs to be anchored firmly in the strategic planning of the business itself. The next level down is analysis. A model is built of the fundamental data and processes needed to operate the enterprise. From this analysis the need for systems is determined.

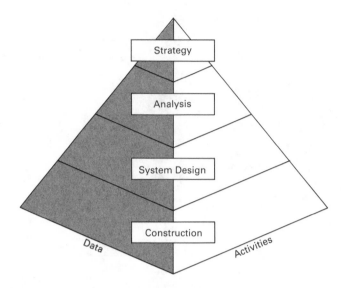

Figure 1.2   Information systems pyramid.

The third layer down relates to system design. The bottom layer relates to the construction of systems.

On the left side of the pyramid are data; on the right are activities. Both the data and activities progress from a high-level, management-oriented view at the top to a fully detailed implementation at the bottom (Fig. 1.3). At the top there must be a strategy concerned with what strategic opportunities exist for making the enterprise more competitive. There must be a strategy relating to future technology and how it could affect the business, its products or services, or its goals and critical success factors. This is important because technology is changing so fast. No enterprise is untouched by the growing power of technology; indeed, some organizations and industries will be changed drastically.

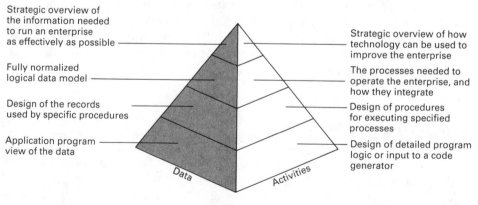

Figure 1.3

Also at the top, there must be strategies for deployment and management of information engineering and of corporate communication networks, both closely tied to availability and adoption of new technologies. The top-level planning needs to guide and prioritize the expenditures on computing so that the information systems (I.S.) department can contribute to the corporate objectives as effectively as possible.

Information engineering applies an engineering-like discipline to all facets and levels of the pyramid, resulting in timely implementation of high-quality systems grounded in the business plans of the enterprise. An engineering-like discipline needs formal techniques. These are implemented with computerized tools, which guide and help the planners, analysts, and implementers. While the tools impose a formality on all stages, they should be designed to maximize the speed with which systems can be built and the ease with which they can be modified.

The disciplines of information engineering are not practical without automated tools. A large amount of knowledge about the enterprise and its systems is collected over an extended period and is constantly updated. This requires a computerized repository with extensive capability for cross-checking and coordinating the knowledge.

It is important that there is a seamless interface between the tools used for each part of the pyramid. The information collected at the higher stages should be used automatically as the analysts and implementers progress to the more detailed stages.

THE MESS IN DATA PROCESSING

Much has been written about what is wrong with data processing today. There are backlogs of several years. It takes too long to build systems, and the cost is too high. The difficulties of maintenance are outrageous. Management cannot obtain information from computers when needed. Tape and disk libraries are a mess of redundant, chaotic data. Many programs are fragile spaghetti code. Problems in data processing prevent the rapid introduction of new business procedures.

Today, computers are assuming more important roles in business, government and the military. We have entered the age when computing and information systems are strategic weapons, not a backroom overhead. The terms *mission-critical system* and *strategic system* have become popular. There are many examples of corporations growing faster than their competition because they had better information systems. In certain cases, corporations have been put out of business by competition with better computing resources. As computing becomes critical to competitive thrusts, it becomes vital both to develop applications quickly and to be able to modify them quickly. Many of today's competitive business thrusts needs require application software far more integrated and complex than that of the past. It is necessary to build—*in a short time, without excessive cost*—applications that are *highly complex,* of *high quality,* and which *truly meet the needs of end users.* These applications must be *easy* and *quick to modify* (maintain).

The Wall Street Journal lamented that software is one of the principal obstacles to economic progress. A former U.S. pentagon chief commented: "If anything kills us before the Russians, it will be our software" [1]. The problems of software development *can* be solved. It is important for executives to realize that there are solutions. A sweeping revolution has begun in the methodologies of putting computers to work. This revolution depends on *power tools.* The methodologies of the past used pencils and templates; the methodologies of the future use design automation techniques linked to code generators, along with computer-aided planning and analysis.

A CRITICAL SUCCESS FACTOR IN BUSINESS

Steadily, corporations are realizing that computers and telecommunications can do much more than automate what was previously done by hand. They are changing the way that corporations do business, changing their relationships with suppliers and customers, changing where decisions are made, changing the organization chart, and creating new strategic alliances among corporations. In some cases entirely new industry patterns are evolving.

The complexity of design of effective computer systems is increasing. It is much more complex to design systems for computer-integrated manufacturing (CIM) than for the isolated manufacturing applications of an earlier era. It is much more complex to provide systems in which customers and suppliers are on-line via networks than the early systems that handle paperwork orders and purchases. The best decision-support systems are much more complex than those of a decade ago. The efficient corporation today is moving to a high level of automation and is highly dependent on computerized information. It is clear that it will have a much higher integration of its computer systems than in the past. A goal of information engineering is to help achieve this integration.

Some corporations have impressive computer systems, designed to give them a competitive advantage, for example, American Airlines with on-line terminals in travel agents' offices or Benetton with its worldwide system, making the world activities "transparent" to the decision makers near Rome. Systems like these have demonstrated how a corporation can pull ahead of its competition by using information and automation better. Efficient corporations will evolve computing systems which are worldwide and exceedingly complex but, nevertheless, which enable procedures to be adapted quickly to changing needs. These complex systems will become an exceedingly important strategic asset of the corporation. To create them requires engineering-like methodologies carried out with automated tools. Simple software engineering is not enough; to build a computerized corporation, we need *information engineering.*

When corporations use network links to customers, suppliers, agents, retailers, and so on, the times for decision-making tend to shorten. Computerized links with suppliers make possible just-in-time inventory management in factories. When buyers for Benetton detect changes in fashion demands in a city, they order clothes to meet that demand. These clothes will be shipped if available, or designed and made quickly, dyed in the fashionable colors, and be in the shops *months before* Benetton's competition with less well computerized systems. A buyer in large but less automated clothing stores cannot compete with the fast-acting Benetton buyer. Using information engineering, First Boston in New York demonstrated that it could bring new financial investment vehicles to market much faster than its Wall Street competition. Nissan Motors in Japan has on-line workstations in car dealers linked with automated production planning and control. With this it can deliver a new car built to a customer's requirements to that customer in two weeks.

Computers and networks between corporations shorten the time span of events. Electronic ordering and electronic mail replace manual ordering and manual mail. The windows of opportunity shorten. As this happens it is necessary to create new procedures *quickly,* or to change existing procedures *quickly.* However, in many organizations today when management needs to change the business procedures or to introduce new products and services, data processing cannot make the required modifications. Application software cannot be changed to keep pace with the dynamic, constantly changing needs of business. A goal of information engineering is to use automated tools within a planned framework in such a way that computerized business procedures can be changed quickly.

To stay competitive in the future, corporations will be dependent on being able to create effective computer applications quickly, and this needs more than tools for designing and building programs. As well as tools, *methodologies* are needed which take advantage of these tools and which harness the knowledge and creativity of computer users. Along with the revolution in power tools, we are likely to see a revolution in development methodology.

The mess in data processing is a serious business problem that *must* be solved. The methodologies of information engineering use computerized planning and analysis to build a knowledgebase which is linked to tools for computer-aided design and code generation.

Replacing the mess in data processing with clean engineering, so that computerized procedures can be built and modified quickly is a *business* critical success factor. It needs to be understood by executives at every level. Top management needs to ensure that its I.S. organization is adapting the new solutions as quickly as possible.

THE NEED FOR POWER TOOLS It would not be possible to build today's cities or microchips or jet aircraft without power tools. Our civilization depends on power tools; yet the applications of computing power to corporate systems is often done by hand methods. Design of the interlocking computer applications of a modern enterprise is no less complex than the design of a microchip or a jet aircraft. To attempt this design by hand methods is to ask for trouble.

The use of power tools changes the methods of construction. Now that such tools exist, it is desirable that the entire application development process be reexamined and improved. Advanced power tools give rise to the need for an engineering-like discipline.

It is important to understand that, as in other industries, power tools change not only the methods of construction but also *what can be constructed*. It is not practical to build highly complex software systems by hand when those systems must change quickly. There is a limit to manual methods. We can observe today extensions of computer applications built because of the use of code generators and nonprocedural languages, I-CASE tools (Chapter 2), knowledge-based technology, and inference engines (Book II).

To stay competitive in the future, corporations will be dependent on power tools for the engineering of information systems. The data processing methodologies of efficient organizations must encompass several new aspects of development technology: application generators, I-CASE tools, fourth-generation languages, information centers, data administration, data modeling, knowledge bases, inference engines, prototyping, strategic information planning, business modeling, automation of the system design process, involvement of end users in design and prototyping, and particularly important, the involvement of top management in the setting of priorities and definition of information needs.

Information engineering links these important approaches to system building into an integrated methodology. The methodology we describe in this book could not have existed before 1985 because it depends on automated tools that require the bit-mapped graphics, mouse, and windows of a powerful personal computer linked to a centralized knowledgebase. These facilities promise to revolutionize the methodology of data processing.

MEAT MACHINES Our human brain is good at some tasks and bad at others. The computer is good at certain tasks that the brain does badly. The challenge of computing is to forge a creative partnership using the best of both.

The electronic machine is fast and absolutely precise. It executes its instructions unerringly. Our meat machine of a brain is slow and usually is not precise. It cannot do long meticulous logic operations without making mistakes. Fortunately, it has some remarkable properties. It can invent, conceptualize, demand improvements, create visions. Humans can write music, start wars, build cities, create art, fall in love, go to the moon, dream of colonizing the solar system, but cannot write COBOL or Ada code guaranteed to be bug-free.

Many of the tasks that information systems (I.S.) professionals do are tasks unsuited to our meat machine brain. They need the precision of an electronic machine. Humans create program specifications that are full of inconsistencies and vagueness. A computer should be helping the human to create specifications and checking them at each step for consistency. It should not be a human job to write programs from the specifications because people cannot do that well. A computer should generate the code needed. When people want to make changes, as they frequently do, they have real problems if they attempt to change the code. A seemingly innocent change has ramifications which they do not perceive and causes a chain reaction of errors.

If the programs needed are large, we are in even worse trouble because we need many people to work together on them. When people try to interact at the level of meticulous detail needed there are all manner of communication errors. When one person makes a change, it affects the work of the others but often the subtle interconnection is not perceived. Meat machines do not communicate with precision.

The end user perceives that the I.S. department has problems but does not know what to do about it. A major part of the problem is that human techniques are slow; I.S. often takes two years to produce results and does not start for a long time because of the backlog. It is rather like communicating with a development team on another solar system where the signals take a year to get there and back.

Of particular concern, the meat machines can handle only a small span of complexity. There is no way that one person or team, unaided, can understand all the systems in a complex enterprise and ensure that they will work together. Today's enterprises are full of inconsistent and uncoordinated programs and files. This is no way to build a computerized corporation. Can you imagine life if the subsystems of your body were inconsistent and uncoordinated—your eye sent signals inconsistent with how your hand worked; your legs were uncoordinated and your lips and tongue did not work well together; information for decision making was in your brain somewhere but the pieces were encoded incompatibly?

In some large banks the capability to do good overall management of customer accounts has been missing because computer systems have been built in an uncoordinated fashion for separate applications such as current accounts, saving accounts, loans, trust, and home mortgages. The data on the separate applications was incompatible. On-line cash management could not be implemented without massive data conversion and system rebuilding.

Following corporate failures in recent years some top executives were unable to obtain answers to vital questions about their own corporation. *Yes,* the data were on the disks, but *no,* the questions could not be answered.

A large commercial volume library has tens of thousands of tapes and disks, most of them containing different types of data items. One commercial application receives data from, or passes data to, many other applications. If these applications are developed without integrated planning of the data, chaos results. Higher management cannot extract data that needs to be drawn from multiple systems. Expensive conversion is needed and often important business options are lost because the data is not available in the right form.

When a corporate president angrily protests that for years he* has been asking for weekly cash balances and is no nearer to receiving them in spite of millions spent on computers and networks, the cause of the problem is that the data needed for such computation is ill-defined and incompatible. The computer world is full of horror stories about information being urgently needed by management or customers but the computers being unable to provide that information even though the requisite data was in their volume library.

An objective of information engineering is to enable a corporation to get its act together. The different systems should be built faster and coordinated with the aid of automation. Information should be planned, designed, coordinated, and made available when needed.

ADVANTAGES   Box 1.2 summarizes the goals and benefits of information engineering.

DIVIDE AND   Building all of the data processing resources that an
CONQUER   enterprise requires is an exceedingly complex undertaking. An objective of information engineering is to make the separate systems relate to one another in an adequate fashion. This does not happen when there is no coordination of the separate development activities. Information engineering therefore starts with a top management view of the enterprise and progresses downward into greater detail (Fig. 1.4).

As the progression into detail occurs, selections must be made concerning which business areas should be analyzed and which systems should be designed. A divide-and-conquer approach is used (Fig. 1.5).

Information engineering begins at the top of an enterprise by conducting an information strategy plan. From this plan a business area is selected for analysis. A portion of the business area is selected for detailed system design. Design automation tools are used for system design, and these tools should link directly to the use of fourth-generation languages or code generators. Thus there are four stages of information engineering, associated with the four levels of the pyramid (Fig. 1.6).

*"He" and "him" are used to imply both genders throughout.

BOX 1.2 Benefits of information engineering

- IE helps to identify strategic systems opportunities and achieve competitive advantage by building such systems before the competition.
- IE focuses data processing on the goals of the business.
- IE enables an enterprise to get its act together. Different systems are coordinated. The same data is represented in the same way in different systems. There is integration among systems where needed.
- IE manages information so that key decision makers can have the best information available.
- New systems can be built relatively quickly, using power tools, within the IE framework.
- IE gives the capability to change computerized procedures quickly.
- IE facilitates the building of systems of greater complexity, and the understanding and control of complex links between systems.
- IE permits the long-term evolution of systems. As systems continue to evolve they become a vital corporate resource.
- IE makes possible major savings through the use of reusable design and code.
- IE drastically reduces the maintenance and backlog problems in enterprises that have converted old systems to IE form.
- A fully computerized enterprise cannot be built without IE techniques.
- Corporations trapped with manually built systems will become increasingly unable to compete with corporations with full information engineering.

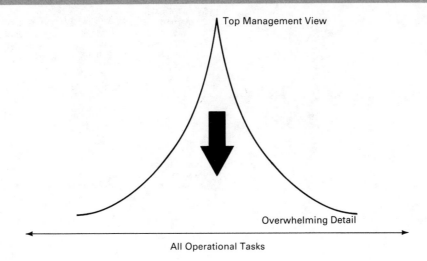

Figure 1.4

11

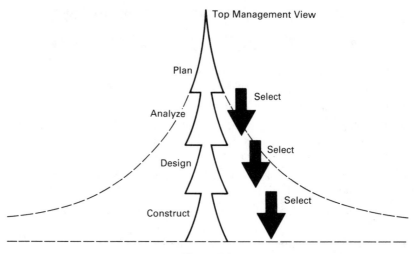

Figure 1.5

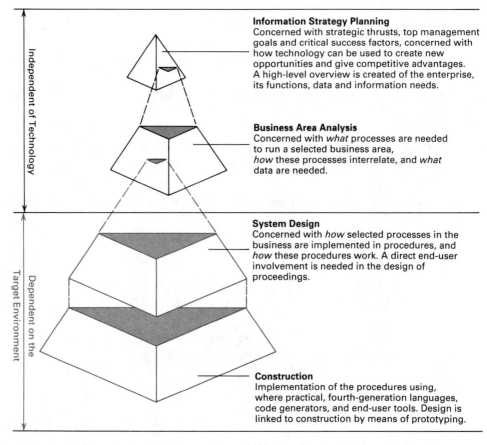

Information Strategy Planning
Concerned with strategic thrusts, top management goals and critical success factors, concerned with how technology can be used to create new opportunities and give competitive advantages. A high-level overview is created of the enterprise, its functions, data and information needs.

Business Area Analysis
Concerned with *what* processes are needed to run a selected business area, *how* these processes interrelate, and *what* data are needed.

System Design
Concerned with *how* selected processes in the business are implemented in procedures, and *how* these procedures work. A direct end-user involvement is needed in the design of proceedings.

Construction
Implementation of the procedures using, where practical, fourth-generation languages, code generators, and end-user tools. Design is linked to construction by means of prototyping.

Figure 1.6 Four stages of information engineering.

THE FOUR STAGES
OF INFORMATION
ENGINEERING

Stage 1: Information Strategy Planning. Concerned with top management goals and critical success factors. Concerned with how technology can be used to create new opportunities or competitive advantages. A high-level overview is created of the enterprise, its functions, data, and information needs.

Stage 2: Business Area Analysis. Concerned with what processes are needed to run a selected business area, how these processes interrelate, and what data is needed.

Stage 3: System Design. Concerned with how selected processes in the business area are implemented in procedures and how these procedures work. Direct end-user involvement is needed in the design of procedures.

Stage 4: Construction. Implementation of the procedures using, where practical, code generators, fourth-generation languages, and end-user tools. Design is linked to construction by means of prototyping.

Stage 1, *information strategy planning,* has taken from three to nine months in most enterprises. It is accomplished by a small team who study the enterprise and interview its management. Information strategy planning requires commitment from top management. A primary concern is that of strategic uses of technology: How can computing be used to make the enterprise more competitive? The results are interesting and stimulating to top management because they are concerned with how technology can be used as a weapon against competition. Diagrammed representations of the enterprise are created which challenge management to think about its structure, its goals, the information needed, and the factors critical for success. The information strategy planning process often results in identification of organizational and operational problems and solutions.

Stage 2, *business area analysis,* is done separately for each business area. A typical business area analysis takes about six months, depending on the breadth of the area selected. Several such studies for different business areas may be done by different teams simultaneously. Business area analysis does not attempt to design systems; it merely attempts to understand and model the processes and data required to run the business area.

Stage 3, *system design,* changes dramatically when design automation tools are used. With these tools, design work is accelerated because the design is created on a computer screen rather than at a drawing board with pencils and plastic templates. The designer can constantly edit the design, adding and changing blocks and links, cutting and pasting, and enhancing detail. The computer provides details about data and processes, guides the designer, and verifies the design through integrity checks. The designer must create a well-structured design; the tools *enforce* this. The tools should require designs that provide a basis for code generation.

Stage 4, *construction,* follows when the computer constructs systems by employing a code generator and sometimes fourth-generation languages or decision-support tools.

It is important to note that the four-stage information engineering process described here requires that much more time be spent on planning and design than on execution. In traditional systems development, time and effort are heavily skewed to coding. This creates a ''chicken-and-egg'' problem, miring I.S. professionals deeper into the development backlog: an endless cycle of poor planning feeding inadequate design, resulting in systems that do not meet business needs and require major revisions and maintenance (i.e., *more coding*). The lack of automated tools for systems development has aggravated this problem. A key objective of information engineering is to impose rules on analysis and design that are formal enough to direct the computer to generate code, thus freeing the I.S. professional from the burden of coding. Systems development under the information engineering discipline attacks the backlog problem from two directions: Planning and rigor result in (1) better systems requiring less revision and maintenance, and (2) breakthroughs in applying computing power to code generation. Systems built under the information engineering discipline should then continue to evolve with business needs on an ongoing basis.

THE ENCYCLOPEDIA   The heart of information engineering is an encyclopedia. The encyclopedia is a computerized repository which steadily accumulates information relating to the planning, analysis, design, construction, and later, maintenance of systems. Tools for computer-aided systems engineering (CASE) and information engineering have employed two types of repository, a dictionary and an encyclopedia.

- A *dictionary* contains names and descriptions of data items, processes, variables, and so on.
- An *encyclopedia* contains this dictionary information and a complete, coded representation of plans, models, and designs, with tools for cross-checking, correlation analysis, and validation. The encyclopedia stores the meaning represented in diagrams and enforces consistency within this representation. The encyclopedia ''understands'' the design, whereas a simple dictionary does not (Box 1.3).

As the stages of information engineering progress, knowledge is gathered and stored in an encyclopedia. The concept of the encyclopedia is central to information engineering. The data models and process models, and planning information are stored in the encyclopedia, as well as facts, rules, and policies

BOX 1.3

A *dictionary* contains names and descriptions of data items, processes, variables, and so on. An *encyclopedia* contains complete coded representations of plans, models, and designs with tools for cross-checking, correlation analysis, and validation. Graphic representations are derived from the encyclopedia and are used to update it. The encyclopedia contains many rules relating to the knowledge it stores and employs rule processing, the artificial-intelligence technique, to help achieve accuracy, integrity, and completeness of the plans, models, and designs. The encyclopedia is thus a *knowledge-base* which not only stores development information but helps control its accuracy and validity.

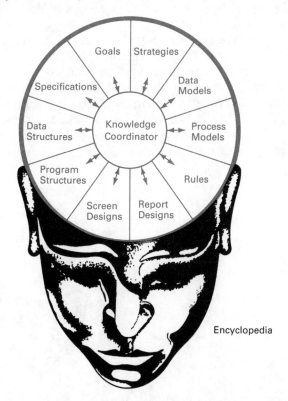

Encyclopedia

The encyclopedia should be designed to drive a code generator. The tool set helps the systems analyst build up in the encyclopedia the information necessary for code generation. To emphasize that the encyclopedia is an intelligent facility which uses rules (in the artificial-intelligence sense) to help achieve accuracy, integrity, and completeness of the plans, models, and designs, it is drawn through these books with the icon shown above.

governing the enterprise and its systems. The encyclopedia is built up steadily as an enterprise practices information engineering (Fig. 1.7).

The encyclopedia stores the meaning represented in diagrams and enforces consistency within this representation. Graphic representations are derived from the encyclopedia and are used to update it by means of CASE tools as described in Chapter 2. The encyclopedia contains many rules relating to the knowledge it stores and employs *rule processing,* an artificial intelligence technique, to help achieve accuracy, integrity, and completeness of the plans, models, and designs. The encyclopedia is thus a *knowledgebase,* which not only stores development information but helps control its accuracy and validity.

Any diagram on a CASE tool screen is a facet of a broader set of knowledge which may reside in the encyclopedia. The encyclopedia normally contains far more detail than is on the diagram. This detail can be displayed in windows by mouse navigation around a hyperdiagram.

At the top of the pyramid, the information in the encyclopedia relates to the strategic planning of the enterprise. The information engineering methodology at this level is more business planning than data processing planning. The intent is to anchor firmly the use of computers into the top management strategies for the enterprise, and to align system development priorities with business strategy priorities (Fig. 1.8). Particularly important are the identification of opportunities by which technology can make the enterprise more competitive. Critical success factors are stored in the encyclopedia and related to other aspects

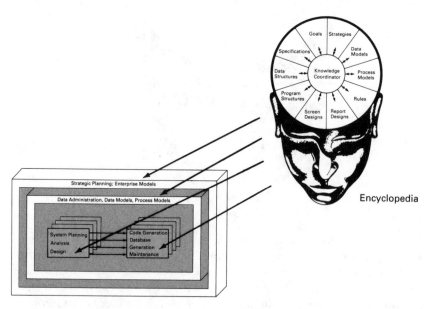

Figure 1.7 The encyclopedia interrelates all parts of the information engineering process.

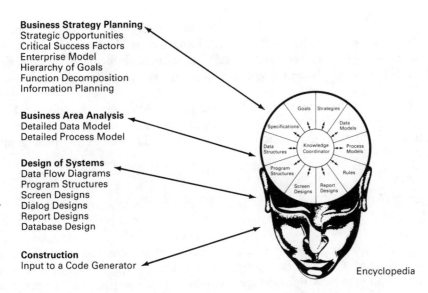

Business Strategy Planning
Strategic Opportunities
Critical Success Factors
Enterprise Model
Hierarchy of Goals
Function Decomposition
Information Planning

Business Area Analysis
Detailed Data Model
Detailed Process Model

Design of Systems
Data Flow Diagrams
Program Structures
Screen Designs
Dialog Designs
Report Designs
Database Design

Construction
Input to a Code Generator

Encyclopedia

Figure 1.8 By means of CASE tools information about the enterprise, its strategic planning, data models, process models, and system designs are built up in the encyclopedia. The encyclopedia should drive a code generator.

of information system planning (as described in Book II). At the analysis level, data models and process models are built up in the encyclopedia.

The design stage uses the information in the encyclopedia to help generate a design. Details of screens, dialogs, reports, program structures, and database structures are built up in the encyclopedia.

In an integrated-CASE (I-CASE) toolset the encyclopedia drives a code generator. The goal of the design workbench is to collect sufficient information that code for the system can be generated. The generator should also generate database description code and job control language. It should generate a comprehensive set of documentation so that designers and maintenance staff can understand the system clearly. It is desirable to select tools that enable implementers to build or generate applications as quickly as possible using a computerized data model.

A high-level overview of the data is created at the top level of the pyramid. This overview is a diagram of the entity types in the corporation and the relationships among these entities—an entity-relationship diagram. Later, details of the attributes are added and a fully normalized data model is built. This model is usually created for one business area at a time. It is part of the work of business area analysis, stage 2 of information engineering.

The entities in an enterprise are identified during the first stage of information engineering. Initially, there is no attempt to identify attributes or to normalize the model. The initial requirement is an overview of the data across the entire enterprise (or the portion of it selected for study).

Many corporations today have fully normalized data models. Preparing these models has been the task of data administrators. Corporations with data models are now linking them into the broader scope of information engineering. System design proceeds with automated tools using the information in the data model.

From an overall logical model of the data in an enterprise, submodels are extracted for the design of specific systems. During the design phase, the data structure is adapted to the capabilities of a specific database or file management system.

COMPUTERIZED DIAGRAMS

A principle of information engineering is that diagrams are the main form of communication between designers and planners and the encyclopedia. The diagrams are built and displayed on a workstation screen. The workstation interacts with analysts, planners, designers, and users to provide *computer-aided design*. Through means of zooming, windowing, nesting, and other computer techniques, the workstation can handle what would become, if drawn on paper, excessively large diagrams.

Diagrams are used for exploring the complex contents of the encyclopedia and for extracting useful components of a design from it. They are the input interface for adding to and modifying the encyclopedia (Fig. 1.9).

Engineering-like disciplines are based on formal techniques. Applying formal techniques to the complex, time-sensitive requirements of modern business is not practical without automated tools. Automated tools impose formality, increase the speed at which systems can be built and modified, and coordinate the vast amount of knowledge that must be collected and updated. Information collected at higher levels of the pyramid can be used automatically as analysts and implementers progress to the more detailed stages.

THE DATA MODEL

An essential foundation block in information engineering is the data model. The logical representation of data can be designed to be relatively *stable*. The stable data model, designed with formal techniques, is a keystone supporting other elements of the information engineering process.

The word *entity* means anything about which we store information (e.g., a customer, supplier, machine tool, employee, utility pole, airline seat, etc.). The entity types of interest to a corporation do not change much with time, nor do the associations among entity types. For each entity type, certain attributes are stored. The attributes relating to a given entity do not change much with time. In practice, it has been found that certain computerized data modeling techniques have been successful in creating a *stable*, logical representation of the data in an enterprise.

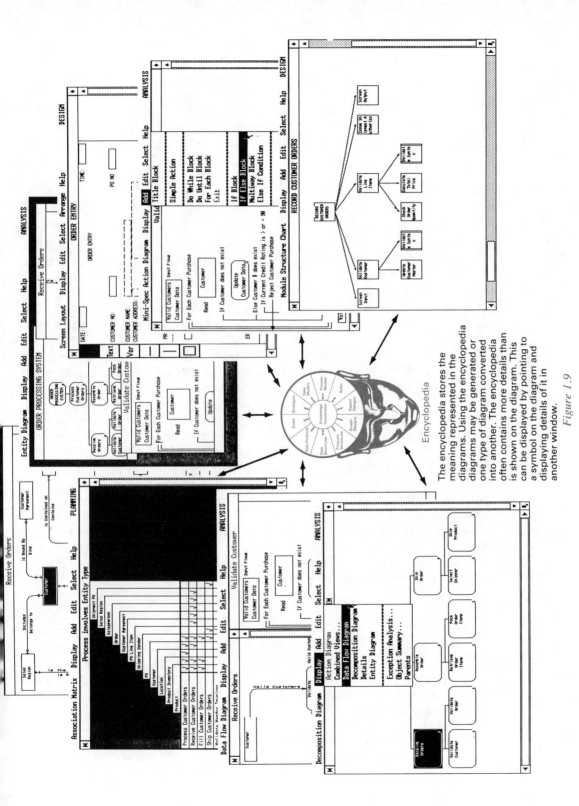

Encyclopedia

The encyclopedia stores the meaning represented in the diagrams. Using the encyclopedia diagrams may be generated or one type of diagram converted into another. The encyclopedia often contains more details than is shown on the diagram. This can be displayed by pointing to a symbol on the diagram and displaying details of it in another window.

Figure 1.9

19

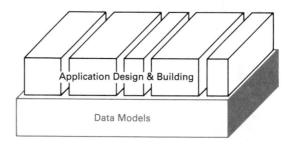

Application Design & Building

Data Models

Figure 1.10

Although the data model is relatively stable, the procedures that use the model change frequently. It is desirable that processes be easily changed because a business needs to be dynamic, constantly striving for better procedures. In information engineering, stable (fully normalized) data models are built with the aid of computerized tools. Applications are built on top of the data models (Fig. 1.10).

At each stage of information engineering, the information gathered is stored in a highly structured fashion in the encyclopedia. This computerized repository of knowledge about the enterprise steadily grows. The knowledge in the encyclopedia is used to help top management in planning and setting priorities, and to help I.S. in performing detailed analysis and design and guiding end-user computing and code generation. The encyclopedia is designed so that the computerized knowledge of the corporation is easily updated.

The encyclopedia-based tools are made as easy to use as possible through automated diagramming. The software guides the user in building the diagrams and entering the requisite information for each stage. The diagrams are easy to modify on the screen.

The encyclopedia is a complex knowledgebase which stores many different types of rules relating to the data. The encyclopedia uses artificial intelligence techniques in its knowledge coordination to ensure that the requisite information is gathered, validated, and cross-coordinated.

ENGINEERING-LIKE TOOLS   The tools and techniques of the past have not had an engineering-like discipline and have not been integrated across all aspects of the pyramid. C. A. R. Hoare, professor of computing at Oxford University, describes the methodologies of conventional data processing as follows:

> The attempt to build a discipline of software engineering on such shoddy foundations must surely be doomed, like trying to base chemical engineering on phlogiston theory, or astronomy on the assumption of a flat earth.[2]

Information engineering recognizes that there is a formal and rigorous way to model data. Data models are built with the aid of computerized tools. In association with the data models, the processes of an enterprise are analyzed formally and linked to the data model. All systems created link to the computerized models of the enterprise and its data. These systems are created with fully structured techniques, again with computerized tools speeding up the process and enforcing discipline. Instead of an ad hoc gaggle of separately conceived applications built with spaghetti-like code, information engineering aims to produce a set of fully structured and easily modified systems based on common models of the enterprise and its data.

In information engineering knowledge needs to be communicated to the encyclopedia via diagrams. The magnitude of the diagrammatic requirements dictates that automated tools are used. The software can apply many powerful checks to the diagrams. The computer stores the *meaning* of the diagrams rather than the pictorial image and so can cross-correlate different types of diagrams relating to the same design. There are many links between the meaning of different diagrams that can be checked with rule-processing techniques.

In one Swiss bank an information engineering team was attempting to draw a diagram showing the procedures at a detailed level. It proved extremely difficult to find the requisite detail because the procedures were performed in computers. The staff who had created the computer system had left, and the staff who had conducted the procedures manually before computerization had also left. The computerized procedures had documentation but it was unstructured Swiss-language documentation that clearly did not represent how the programs worked today. Programmers often distrust external documentation and deviate from it when they are doing maintenance. The documentation slips into disuse. As programs grow old in an organization it is easy to use them but forget how their internals work. Their internals often have patches on top of patches on top of patches with no trustworthy documentation. One can imagine an enterprise 20 years from now, its computer programs immensely complex but nobody really understanding how they work.

To prevent such a scenario, the enterprise needs to have its data and procedures represented in an encyclopedia, which is a living facility rather than dead paperwork. Modifications to systems in an automated environment take place by adjusting the design in the encyclopedia and regenerating code. The clearly structured knowledge in the encyclopedia is vital for understanding and modifying complex systems. The designs need to be displayable with graphics that are as easy to understand and modify as possible.

END-USER PARTICIPATION

A particularly important characteristic of information engineering is that end users participate in each stage. At the top of the pyramid, top management is involved in establishing goals and critical success factors. Management helps determine what information is needed from computers and sets priorities for development. At the second level, senior end users help to create and validate the data models and process models. At the design stage, end users are involved in joint application design sessions and often employ the easy-to-use graphic representations of specifications. Design merges into implementation as prototypes are created and used. In an information center environment, the users may build their own systems, with the help of the information in the encyclopedia.

Clear easy-to-understand diagrams are essential for end-user participation. Sessions with end users and management sometimes take place in a meeting room with a large-screen projector displaying the workstation screen. The styles of computerized diagramming need to be designed for end-user comprehension. A high level of creativity is often evident when end users learn the language of system design and are encouraged to invent how computers could help them streamline procedures, cut head count, expand sales, simplify work, or make better decisions.

FOURTH-GENERATION LANGUAGES

Since 1980 many new languages have come into use which increase the speed of building systems or analyzing data [3]. These languages are of a variety of types:

- *End-user languages,* enabling users who are not professional programmers to query databases, generate reports, perform elaborate calculations, and create simple systems.

- *Decision-support languages,* enabling users to build business models for decision making, manipulate spreadsheets, and generate charts.

- *Fourth-generation programming languages,* enabling programs to be written with a fraction of number of lines of code and in a fraction of the time that would be needed with COBOL, PL/I, and so on.

- *Nonprocedural languages,* which put a computer to work by stating *what* is wanted rather than *how* to do it.

- *Prototyping languages,* which enable a prototype to be created quickly and modified quickly, so that end users can employ it, react to it, and have it adjusted to their needs.

- *Rule-based languages,* for creating expert systems or other systems where the drawing of inferences from many rules is needed.

A goal of information engineering is that high-productivity languages should be used wherever practical for prototyping, end-user computing, speeding up professional I.S. development, and making maintenance easier. Among the most powerful productivity aids are code generators, which should be driven directly from the screen of the CASE tool.

EIGHT TRENDS   There is a constant ongoing search for better metho-
                dologies in data processing. Eight types of approach
have been advocated by different authorities, and any one of the eight is valuable in itself. The *integration* of the eight approaches makes all of them more
valuable. Information engineering creates a synthesis of them (Fig. 1.11). The
eight trends are as follows:

1. Strategic Planning of Information Systems

This trend seeks to relate the use of computers in an enterprise to top management needs and perspectives. It is concerned with formalizing management
goals and critical success factors, modeling the enterprise, and strategic planning of information and its use. Particularly important, it should identify ways
in which the enterprise can change, or use technology differently, to achieve
competitive thrusts.

2. Data-Centered Design

This set of techniques is concerned with formal data administration and data
modeling. Systems have proven to be much easier to build and much cheaper
to maintain when thorough data modeling has been completed. It is impractical
to maintain control of application building without computerized data models.

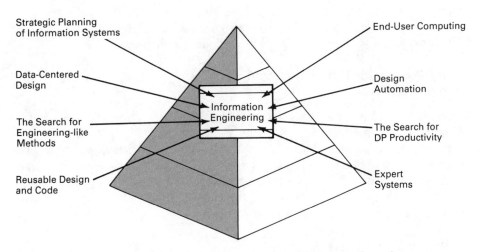

Figure 1.11 Each of these eight thrusts in the methodology of creating systems is valuable in itself. Information engineering synthesizes them into one
methodology.

3. The Search for Engineering-like Methods

Conventional structured techniques improved the design of systems but did not go far enough. More rigorous techniques are possible when computers are used to help build specifications and link them into computerized models of data. Computers can perform comprehensive cross-checks throughout a complex system. As hand methodologies are replaced with computerized methodologies, more rigorous engineering-like techniques that would be too tedious to attempt by hand are possible.

4. End-User Computing

The end-user revolution in computing has spread rapidly in some corporations (but not others). Many organizations have information centers and numerous end-user tools. Creating prototypes that end users can critique has been common in system building. Analysts guide end users through joint application design sessions in order to specify what systems are needed. It has become clear that techniques are needed for guiding end-user computing to prevent a *Tower of Babel* from springing up as a result of randomly designed data and redundant procedures. Information engineering is perceived as a necessary guidance mechanism.

5. Design Automation

Computer-aided design techniques have spread rapidly in mechanical and electronic engineering. They are even more critical to systems engineering. Diagrams for all aspects of systems engineering can be built at a workstation screen, with the computer aiding the designer and checking the design. CASE tools for doing this should be the basis of code generators.

6. The Search for Data Processing Productivity

The building of data processing systems takes too long. Time and cost overruns are normal. The maintenance problems are intolerable. Major attacks on these problems have been made by means of fourth-generation languages, application generators, prototyping tools, and end-user tools. In some cases, these have dramatically improved data processing productivity. The coupling of design automation tools to code generators is especially important for improving the speed and quality of systems building.

7. Reusable Design and Code

Most analysts and programmers are creating designs and code that have been created thousands of times before. It is desirable to find techniques for reusing designs and code, and making them easy to modify where necessary. Information engineering's top-down approach can identify processes that are used many times in the enterprise. The designs for these should be reused and the code generated. In some enterprises this has brought great savings in implementation.

8. Expert Systems

Expert systems are a spin-off from artificial-intelligence research. They apply inference processing to a knowledge base which contains data and rules, in order to make a computer emulate human expertise and sometimes to build up a level of expertise more precise and comprehensive than any one human could achieve. Information engineering should use expert system techniques to help planners, analysts, and designers create better systems.

Information engineering attempts to integrate these eight trends and to create one encyclopedia that relates to all the trends.

CONCLUSION

Early experience with information engineering has shown that once the data models are built, the construction of systems proceeds much more quickly. A period of initial effort is needed before the major payoff occurs. Now that better tools are available with comprehensive encyclopedia software, the initial planning is improving, and the construction of systems is accelerating. *Design automation linked to code generation* results in extremely high productivity compared to that of traditional data processing techniques.

The real needs of end users are much more likely to be met, for several reasons:

- The end users are involved in planning their information needs.
- The end users are employed in joint application design sessions.
- Prototypes are created and can rapidly be changed.
- Systems can be built faster and modified more easily.
- Information center tools are used.

Information engineering integrates those techniques that can avoid the spaghetti-like mess of the past (Fig. 1.12). The encyclopedia and CASE tools not only enforce design rigor but coordinate the design and interfaces across an enterprise so that the different parts work together.

Information engineering differs from traditional structured techniques in the following ways:

- It creates a framework for developing a computerized enterprise.
- Separately developed systems fit into this framework.

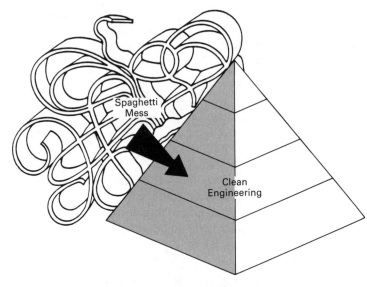

Spaghetti
Mess

Clean
Engineering

Figure 1.12

- It concentrates on the enterprise goals and needs.
- It integrates analysis and design across a corporation. It is thus much broader in scope than software engineering.
- It maximizes the opportunities for reusable design and code.
- It is based on formal data models.
- It is designed for code generators.
- It is designed for automated techniques, which can handle a degree of complexity not practical with manual techniques.
- It guides the planners, analysts, and designers with fill-in screens.
- The encyclopedia steadily accumulates knowledge about the enterprise and its systems.

To succeed fully, information engineering needs top management commitment; it is a corporate-wide activity that needs firm direction from the top. The methodology relates to top management planning.

It would be unthinkable to build a space shuttle without an overall plan. Once the overall plan exists, however, separate teams can go to work on the components. Corporate information systems development is not much less complex than building a space shuttle, yet in most corporations it is done without an overall plan of sufficient detail to make the components fit together.

The overall architect of the shuttle cannot conceivably specify the detailed design of the rockets, electronics, or other subsystems. These details have to be developed by different teams working autonomously. Imagine, however, what would happen if these teams enthusiastically created their own subsystems without any coordination from the top. The data processing world is full of inspired subsystem builders, who want to be left alone. Their numbers are rapidly increasing as small computers proliferate and end users learn to acquire their own facilities. There is all the difference in the world between a corporation with computing that fits into an overall architecture and a corporation with incompatible systems.

It is the job of every top executive today to build a computerized enterprise, and a computerized enterprise cannot be created effectively without information engineering.

REFERENCES

1. *Atherton Technology White Paper,* Atherton Technology, Sunnyvale, CA, Aug. 1987.

2. C. A. R. Hoare, *The Engineering of Software: A Startling Contradiction,* Computer Bulletin, British Computer Society, Dec. 1975.

3. James Martin, *Fourth-Generation Languages,* Volume I: *Principles,* Prentice-Hall, Inc., Englewood Cliffs, NJ, 1985.

2 CASE AND I-CASE

INTRODUCTION   The first attempts at information engineering were carried out before today's computerized tools existed. While the pioneers demonstrated the potential of information engineering, they showed that it really needs automation. In the mid-1980s the term CASE (computer-aided software engineering) became popular to describe power tools for the systems analyst. Some of these tools were narrow in scope, so the term I-CASE, *integrated CASE,* is used to describe toolkits in which tools for all aspects of software development are integrated [1].

The systems analyst interacts with a CASE tool by means of diagrams (Fig. 2.1). Diagrams are used to represent planning information, an overview of systems, data models and data flows, detailed designs, and program structures. A principle of CASE is that whenever possible diagrams are used as an aid to clear thinking. The figures in this chapter show examples of the types of diagrams that I.S. professionals create on a workstation screen with CASE tools.

A critical characteristic of an I-CASE tool (as opposed to merely "CASE") is that it generates executable programs. A code generator is driven by the design workbench. The tight integration of the analysis and design tools with a code generator gives much higher productivity than these tools when they are not coupled.

In the past, systems analysts drew their diagrams with pencils and erasers (Fig. 2.2). Often, hand-drawn diagrams became very large, straggling across white boards or pasted onto large sheets of paper. A design often had binders of nested data-flow diagrams and structure charts. These binders contained numerous errors, inconsistencies, and omissions which were not caught. Often, the diagrams themselves were sloppy and the diagramming technique casual or ill-thought-out.

CASE tools enforce precision in diagramming. A good CASE tool employs diagram types which are precise and computer-checkable. Large complex

Figure 2.1 Analysts working at the screen of an information-engineering workbench—the IEF from Texas Instruments.

diagrams can be handled by means of zooming, nesting, windowing, and other computer techniques. The computer quickly catches errors and inconsistencies even in very large sets of diagrams. Today, business, government, and the military need highly complex and integrated computer applications. The size and complexity are too great for there to be any hope of accurate diagramming without the aid of a computer. The magnitude of the diagrammatic requirements for information engineering dictates that automated tools be used.

It is the *meaning* represented by the diagram, rather than its graphic image, which is valuable. A good CASE tool stores that meaning in a computer-processible form. The tool helps build up a design, data model, or other deliverable segment of the development process in such a way that it can be validated and then used in a subsequent development stage.

OBJECTS AND ASSOCIATIONS   Many CASE diagrams show *objects* and *associations* among objects. The objects are drawn as boxes on a diagram and the associations are drawn as lines connecting the boxes. Examples of objects are:

- An entity type
- A process
- A data store
- A program module

Figure 2.2 Hand-drawn diagrams usually contain inconsistencies, errors, and omissions, which a CASE tool could detect. They are slow to draw and cumbersome to revise, so that they inhibit experimenting with design changes. Hand-drawn diagrams are entirely inadequate as a basis for complex systems or for an information engineering approach.

- A department
- A business goal

Examples of associations are:

- A relationship between two entity types
- A data flow on a data-flow diagram
- A parent–child association on a decomposition diagram

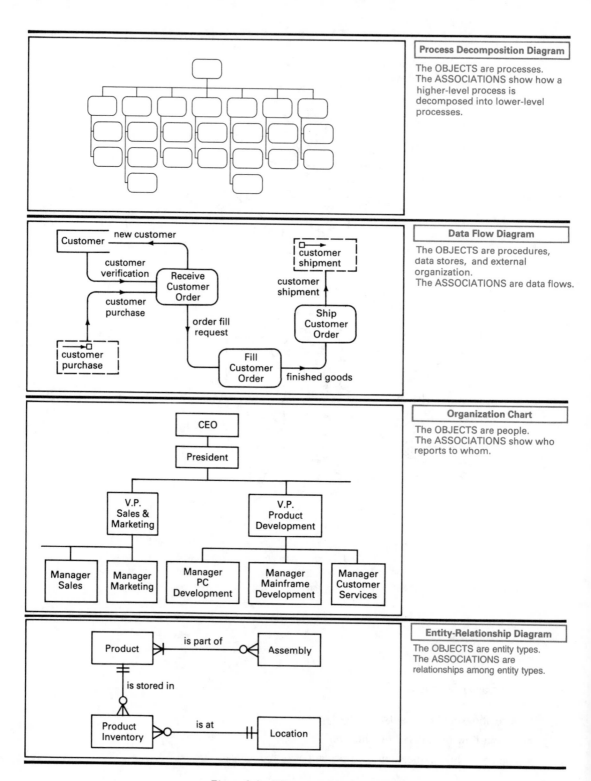

Process Decomposition Diagram

The OBJECTS are processes. The ASSOCIATIONS show how a higher-level process is decomposed into lower-level processes.

Data Flow Diagram

The OBJECTS are procedures, data stores, and external organization. The ASSOCIATIONS are data flows.

Organization Chart

The OBJECTS are people. The ASSOCIATIONS show who reports to whom.

Entity-Relationship Diagram

The OBJECTS are entity types. The ASSOCIATIONS are relationships among entity types.

Figure 2.3 Diagrams with objects and associations.

- A line showing how a procedure is dependent on other procedures
- A line connecting events on a PERT chart

Figure 2.3 shows diagrams with objects and associations. The CASE software may ask the user for detailed information about each object and each association. When needed, this information is entered or displayed in *windows*. Figure 2.4 shows an example of a window appearing on a CASE diagram. By means of such windows, the CASE software should collect a complete set of data so that it can check the integrity of models and designs, do design calculations, and have the information it needs for code generation.

Sometimes the relationships among objects are best displayed with a matrix diagram. Figure 2.5 shows matrix diagrams. Again, details may be entered or displayed using windows. If the user points to a cell in the matrix, a window may appear which would show the details known about that intersection or the details that must be entered.

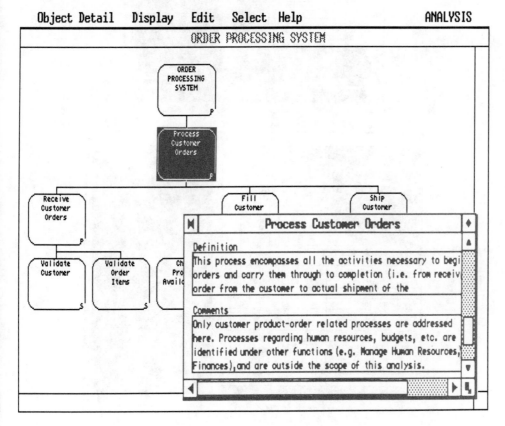

Figure 2.4   A scrollable window on a CASE screen requesting input of specific details.

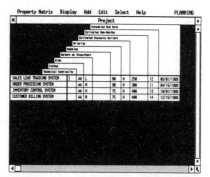

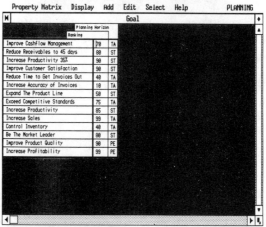

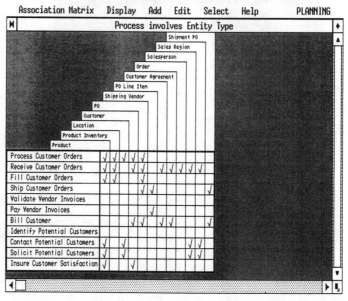

Figure 2.5 Three matrix diagrams.

DIAGRAMS OF PROGRAMS

A particularly important form of diagram is that which shows the structure of programs. It should represent optimal program structuring and show loops, nesting, conditions, CASE structures, escapes, database accesses, subroutine calls, and other program structures.

Curiously, in the early evolution of structured techniques, no such diagram was used. Perhaps because of this, some of the early CASE tools had no such diagram. Yourdon-style "structure charts" do not show loops, conditions, CASE structures, and so on. A program structure can be made clear by representing it visually in such a way that any portion of it can be either contracted on the screen to examine an overview or expanded to examine detail. Detail can be added to the structure one step at a time.

Figure 2.6 shows an action diagram used for representing a specification. The action diagram can be drawn independently of any programming language or can be set to a particular language. Figure 2.7 shows an action diagram set to COBOL. An action diagram can show the language of a code generator. Commands representing programming constructs need not be typed; they can be selected from a mouse menu. When the computer adds them to the action diagram, it cannot do so with missing END statements or incorrect CASE structures. It can insist that "ELSE" actions are filled in when a condition is used. It can enforce optimal code structuring. Action diagrams are also used to show specifications in a structured form.

A box representing a procedure on a decomposition diagram, data-flow diagram, or other diagram can be expanded in the form of an action diagram. Figure 2.8 shows this. The action diagram shows the data types that are the inputs and outputs of the procedure. Action diagrams are discussed in Books II and III of the trilogy.

THE LANGUAGE OF DIAGRAMS

The diagrams and their manipulation by computer are a form of thought processing. The analyst, designer, programmer, user, and executive need a family of diagram types to assist in clear thinking. These diagram types should be as clear and simple as possible. Although there are many diagram types, a minimum number of icons should have to be learned and their meanings should be as obvious as possible.

The diagrams must be complete enough and rigorous enough to serve as a basis for code generation and for automatic conversion of one type of diagram into another. The diagrams of the early "structured revolution" are not good enough for this. The analyst and designer had to use human intelligence to bridge gaps between one type of diagram and another, and they often made mistakes in doing so. I-CASE needs a complete, integrated, rigorous set of diagramming standards.

Given appropriate diagramming techniques, it is much easier to describe

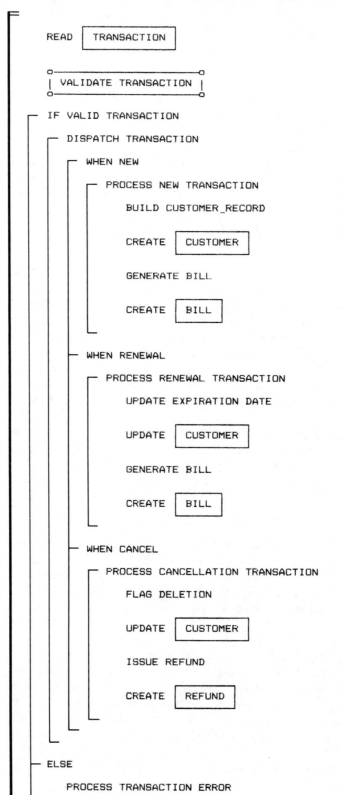

READ [TRANSACTION]

|—o——————————o
| | VALIDATE TRANSACTION |
|—o——————————o

IF VALID TRANSACTION

   DISPATCH TRANSACTION

      WHEN NEW

         PROCESS NEW TRANSACTION

            BUILD CUSTOMER_RECORD

            CREATE [CUSTOMER]

            GENERATE BILL

            CREATE [BILL]

      WHEN RENEWAL

         PROCESS RENEWAL TRANSACTION

            UPDATE EXPIRATION DATE

            UPDATE [CUSTOMER]

            GENERATE BILL

            CREATE [BILL]

      WHEN CANCEL

         PROCESS CANCELLATION TRANSACTION

            FLAG DELETION

            UPDATE [CUSTOMER]

            ISSUE REFUND

            CREATE [REFUND]

ELSE

   PROCESS TRANSACTION ERROR

Figure 2.6 Action diagram of a specification.

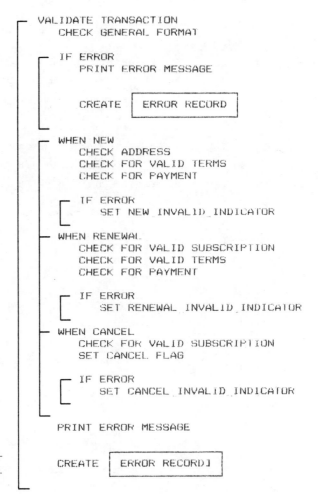

Figure 2.6a The block VALI-
DATE TRANSACTION, in Fig.
2.6, expanded into more detail.

complex activities and procedures in diagrams than in text. A picture can be much better than a thousand words because it is concise, precise, and clear. Computerized diagrams do not allow the sloppiness and woolly thinking common in textual specifications.

Engineers of different types all use formal diagrams that are precise in meaning: mechanical drawings, architects' drawings, circuit diagrams, microelectronics designs, and so on. Software engineering and information engineering also need formal diagrams with standardized diagramming constructs.

As in other branches of engineering, the diagrams become the documentation for systems (along with the additional information collected in the encyclopedia when the diagrams are drawn). When changes are made to systems,

TEXAS INSTRUMENTS
PROCESS ACTION DIAGRAM (PAD)

Procedure Step: MAINTAIN_DETAIL

```
 1-  ┌─ MAINTAIN_DETAIL
 2-  │   IMPORTS:  Entity View input_display work_area
 3-  │             Group View  input_group
 4-  │             Entity View input_time
 5-  │             Entity View input_schedule
 6-  │             Entity View input_executive
 7-  │   EXPORTS:  Entity View output_display work_area
 8-  │             Group View  group_output
 9-  │             Entity View output_time
10-  │             Entity View output_schedule
11-  │             Entity View output_executive
12-  │   ENTITY ACTIONS: Entity View action attendee
13-  │                   Entity View action time
14-  │                   Entity View action schedule
15-  │                   Entity View action executive
16-  │   MOVE input_display work_area  TO output_display work_area
17-  │   MOVE input_time  TO output_time
18-  │   MOVE input_schedule  TO output_schedule
19-  │   MOVE input_executive  TO output_executive
20-  │   ┌─ IF COMMAND IS EQUAL TO rtnrevw
21-  │   │  EXIT STATE IS return_to_review_schedule
22- <─┼───└─ESCAPE
23-  │   └─
24-  │   ┌─ FOR EACH input_group
25-  │   │     TARGETING group_output FROM THE BEGINNING UNTIL FULL
26-  │   └─ MOVE input attendee  TO output attendee
27-  │   └─
28-  │   ┌─ READ action executive
29-  │   │      WITH operator_id EQUAL TO input executive operator_id
30-  │   ├─ WHEN not found
31-  │   │  EXIT STATE IS executive_not_found
32- <─┼───└─ESCAPE
33-  │   └─
34-  │   ┌─ READ action schedule
35-  │   │      WITH date EQUAL TO input schedule date
36-  │   │      WHICH is_kept_by THE CURRENT OCCURRENCE OF action
37-  │   │             executive
38-  │   ├─ WHEN not found
39-  │   │  EXIT STATE IS schedule_not_found
40- <─┼───└─ESCAPE
41-  │   └─
42-  │   ┌─ READ action time
43-  │   │      WITH slot EQUAL TO input time slot
44-  │   │      WHICH is_contained_in THE CURRENT OCCURRENCE OF action
45-  │   │             schedule
46-  │   ├─ WHEN not found
47-  │   │  EXIT STATE IS update_time_failure
48- <─┼───└─ESCAPE
49-  │   └─
50-  │   ┌─ CASE OF COMMAND
51-  │   ├─ CASE display
52-  │   │  MOVE action time  TO output time
53-  │   │  USE convert_slot_to_time
54-  │   │     WHICH IMPORTS: Entity View input_display work_area
55-  │   │                    Entity View input_time
56-  │   │     WHICH EXPORTS: Entity View output time
57-  │   │                    Entity View output_display work_area
58-  │   ┌─ READ EACH action attendee
59-  │   │      TARGETING group_output FROM THE BEGINNING UNTIL FULL
60-  │   │      SORTED BY ASCENDING last_name
61-  │   │      WHICH attends THE CURRENT OCCURRENCE OF action time
62-  │   │  MOVE action attendee  TO output attendee
63-  │   │  MAKE output attendee last_name Protected Normal Intensity White
64-  │   │  MAKE output attendee first_name Protected Normal Intensity White
```

Figure 2.7 Action diagram of COBOL code.

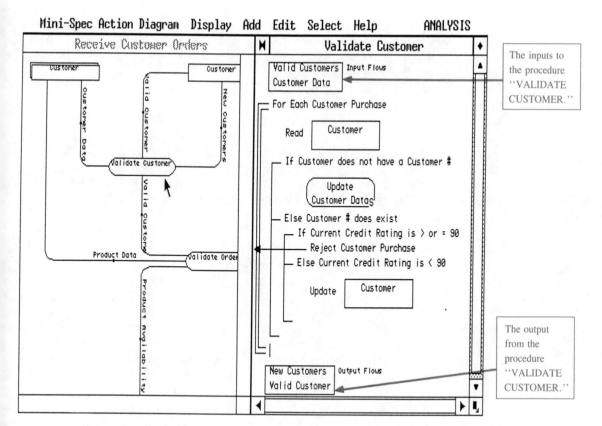

Figure 2.8 Action diagram window showing details of a block on a data-flow diagram. The top and bottom of the action diagram indicate the input data and output data. These must correspond to the information on the data-flow diagram. (Courtesy KnowledgeWare)

the diagrams will be changed on the screen, and the code will be regenerated. The design documentation does not then slip out of date as changes are made.

Philosophers have often described how what we are capable of thinking depends on the language we use for thinking. When Roman numerals were in use, ordinary people could not multiply or divide. That capability spread when Arabic numbers became widely used. The diagrams we draw of complex processes are a form of language. With computers, we may want to create processes more complex than those we would perform manually. Appropriate diagrams help us to visualize and invent those processes.

- *For a person developing a system design or program, the diagrams used are aids to clear thinking.* A poor choice of diagramming technique can inhibit thinking. A good choice can speed up work and improve the quality of the results.

- *When several people work on a system or program, the diagrams serve as an essential communication tool.* A formal diagramming technique is needed to enable the developers to interchange ideas and make their separate components fit together with precision.

- *When systems are modified, clear diagrams are an essential aid to maintenance.* They make it possible for a new team to understand how the program works and to design changes. When a change is made, it often affects other parts of the program.

- *Clear diagrams of the program structure enable maintenance programmers to understand the consequential effects of changes they make.* When debugging, clear diagrams are also highly valuable tools for understanding how the programs ought to work and for tracking down what might be wrong.

Diagramming, then, is a language essential for both clear thinking and human communication. An enterprise needs standards for its information systems diagrams, just as it has standards for engineering drawings [2].

HYPERDIAGRAMS   A diagram and its associated information in a CASE tool can be very different from that on paper. Paper constrains the diagram to what can be drawn in a two-dimensional space. Analysts are used to building designs with two-dimensional drawings. With a computer, many different representations can be linked together logically. A block on a data-flow diagram may be the same as a block on a decomposition diagram. A data access on an action diagram must relate to information on an entity-relationship diagram or data model. The inputs and outputs to a procedure represented by an action must be the same as those on the corresponding data-flow diagram.

The analyst using the screen of a CASE tool may point at a block or line and display details of that block or line. The details may be displayed in the form of another diagram, sometimes a diagram of a different type. They may be displayed in the form of text or fill-in-the-blanks panels. The analyst may have multiple windows on the screen at one time, showing different aspects of a design, as shown in Fig. 2.9. He may have a "SHOW-AS" menu (like that in Fig. 2.10) with which he can display different aspects of a design.

The term *hyperdiagram* or *hyperchart* describes a representation of plans, models, or designs in which multiple two-dimensional representations are logically linked together. A simple hyperdiagram is a diagram in which the details of objects may be displayed in windows. A more complex hyperdiagram uses multiple types of two-dimensional diagrams. A block or a line may be displayed in a window as text, as a fill-in-the-blanks form, an action diagram, a matrix, a different type of diagram, and so on.

Figure 2.11 shows a family of screen windows which are part of one hy-

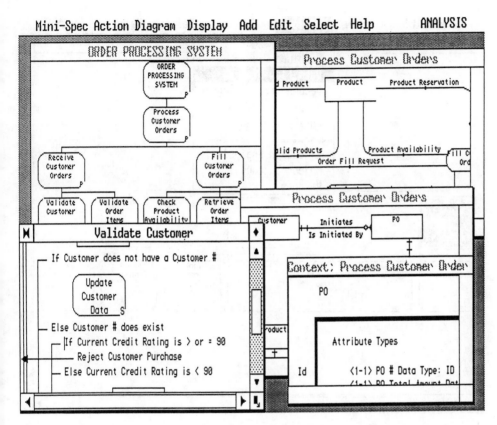

Figure 2.9 Workbench screen with multiple windows. Each window can be scrolled, expanded to fill the screen, and shown with more detail than here.

perdiagram. The hyperdiagram can be explored by pointing to objects or associations and displaying details of them. There can be diagrams within diagrams within diagrams; there can be details within details within details.

A system is generally too complex to draw as a single type of diagram. Its components may be summarized with a decomposition diagram or their interdependencies shown with a data-flow diagram. The detailed logic may be depicted with an action diagram. The system may use a database structure, and individual views of data are derived from that structure. The action diagram may refer to screen designs or report designs. All of these may be stored in a computable form, with explanatory text, in a hyperdiagram. An I-CASE toolkit gives the implementer the facilities to explore or to build the hyperdiagram. *The tool should enforce consistency within the hyperdiagram.*

Figures 2.12 through 2.14 show illustrations of diagrams that are linked to form hyperdiagrams. Because the hyperdiagrams contain logical linkages be-

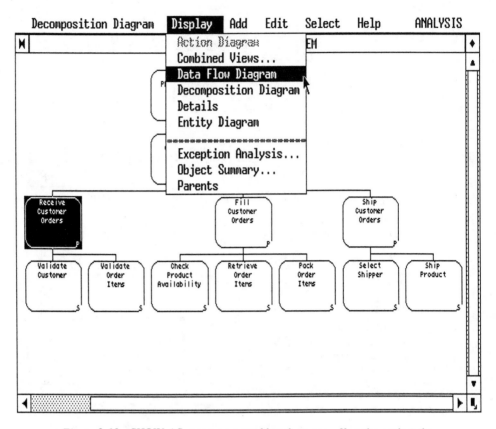

Figure 2.10 SHOW-AS menu on a workbench screen offers the analyst the
choice of different ways of displaying objects or designs. The RECEIVE CUS-
TOMER ORDER block, for example, might be displayed as an action diagram,
data-flow diagram, or decomposition diagram; a window could display its details
or a diagram of the entity-types it uses. (Courtesy KnowledgeWare)

tween different types of representations and enforce consistency among these
representations, they are a major advance on paper-oriented methods of analysis
and design.

**A VITAL
CORPORATE
RESOURCE**
In a complex enterprise using I-CASE development
techniques the encyclopedia grows large, steadily accumulating information about the enterprise and its
systems, its data models, data flows, rules, specifi-
cations, screen designs, and so on. In organizations committed to this approach
it has become an extremely valuable corporate resource.

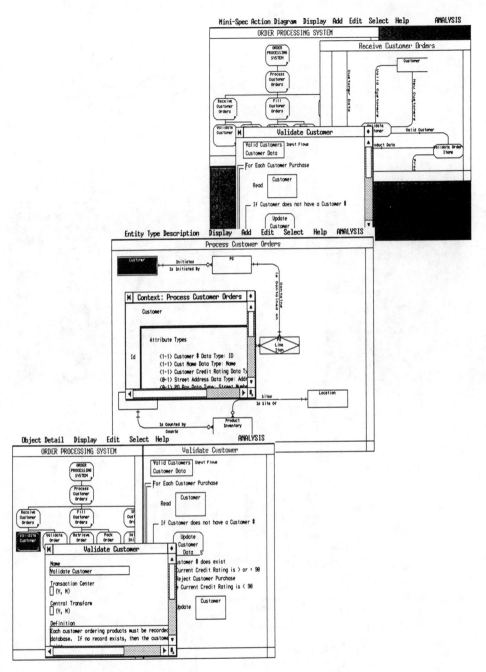

Figure 2.11 All of these diagrams are parts of one hyperdiagram. They are parts of a logically consistent whole. The analyst may examine more information about this hyperdiagram by selecting blocks (or links between blocks) and displaying them in detail windows. The windows can be scrolled or expanded to show more detail than here. The computer enforces consistency within the hyperdiagram and among hyperdiagrams.

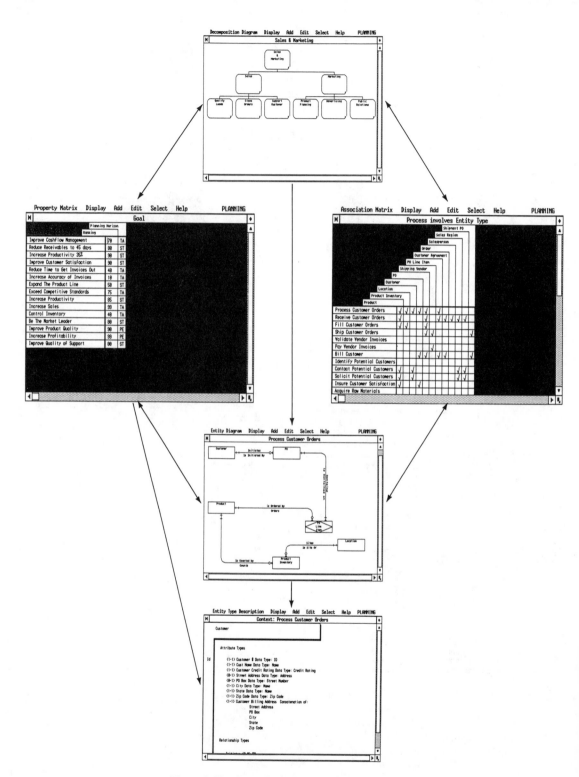

Figure 2.12　Some logical connections in a complex hyperdiagram.

Figure 2.15 shows the encyclopedia accumulating information from the planning, analysis, design, or construction toolkits and generating code, database descriptions and documentation. Structured code is usually not as efficient as highly optimized code. The code may, therefore, be fed into an optimizer to make it as machine efficient as possible (bottom, Fig. 2.15). This diagram encapsulates the nature of an I-CASE toolset.

DISTRIBUTED ARCHITECTURE

Coordinating the knowledge across a large development or information engineering effort requires substantial computing and is likely to be done on the machine that controls the central encyclopedia. Analysts using CASE tools, however, need fast response from their own workstation; so there should be an encyclopedia and knowledge coordinator in that workstation. A distributed architecture is thus desirable.

Figure 2.16 shows the architecture of the KnowledgeWare toolset. The personal computer workstation contains an encyclopedia and knowledge coordinator which ensures consistency among the information provided by different tools that the developer uses. The mainframe contains a central encyclopedia with a knowledge coordinator that controls consistency among the work of different developers. From the central encyclopedia, the developer can check out a *hyperdiagram* or a set of objects, which are then duplicated in his own encyclopedia. He can work with them, creating new information which is coordinated in his own workstation. When he is satisfied with it, he checks it back into the central encyclopedia, where coordination with the central information is carried out. Thus consistency is achieved across a large project or across multiple projects in an information engineering environment. Figure 2.17 shows the architecture of the Texas Instruments IEF (information engineering facility).

Building and integrating the information systems needed in an enterprise are achieved by synthesizing the models and designs of many people scattered across the enterprise. CASE tools with a central encyclopedia make this possible. The amount of complexity of information in an enterprise is so great that synthesis is a practical impossibility *unless computerized tools are used to achieve it*.

The objective is to achieve as much internal consistency as possible in the knowledge in the encyclopedia. In a large organization, complete consistency is unlikely to be achieved, especially early in the evolution of information engineering. The methodology and CASE tools need to be designed to enable an enterprise to work toward consistency, but also to operate with different versions of objects and zones of internal consistency and, possibly, interfaces between zones which are agreed to be inconsistent.

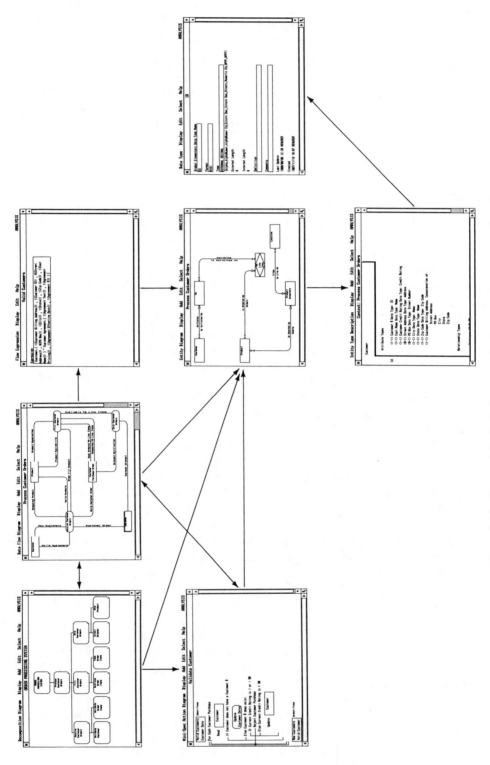

Figure 2.13 Some of the logical connections in a complex hyperdiagram.

46

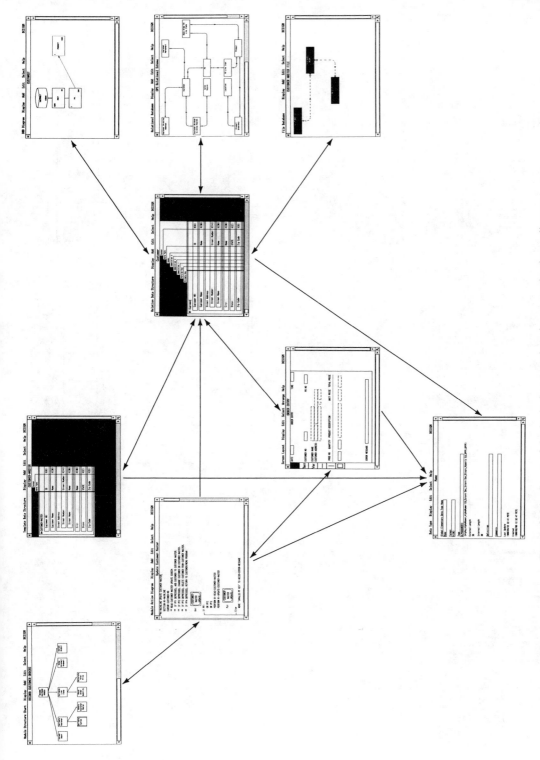

Figure 2.14 Some of the logical connections in a complex hyperdiagram.

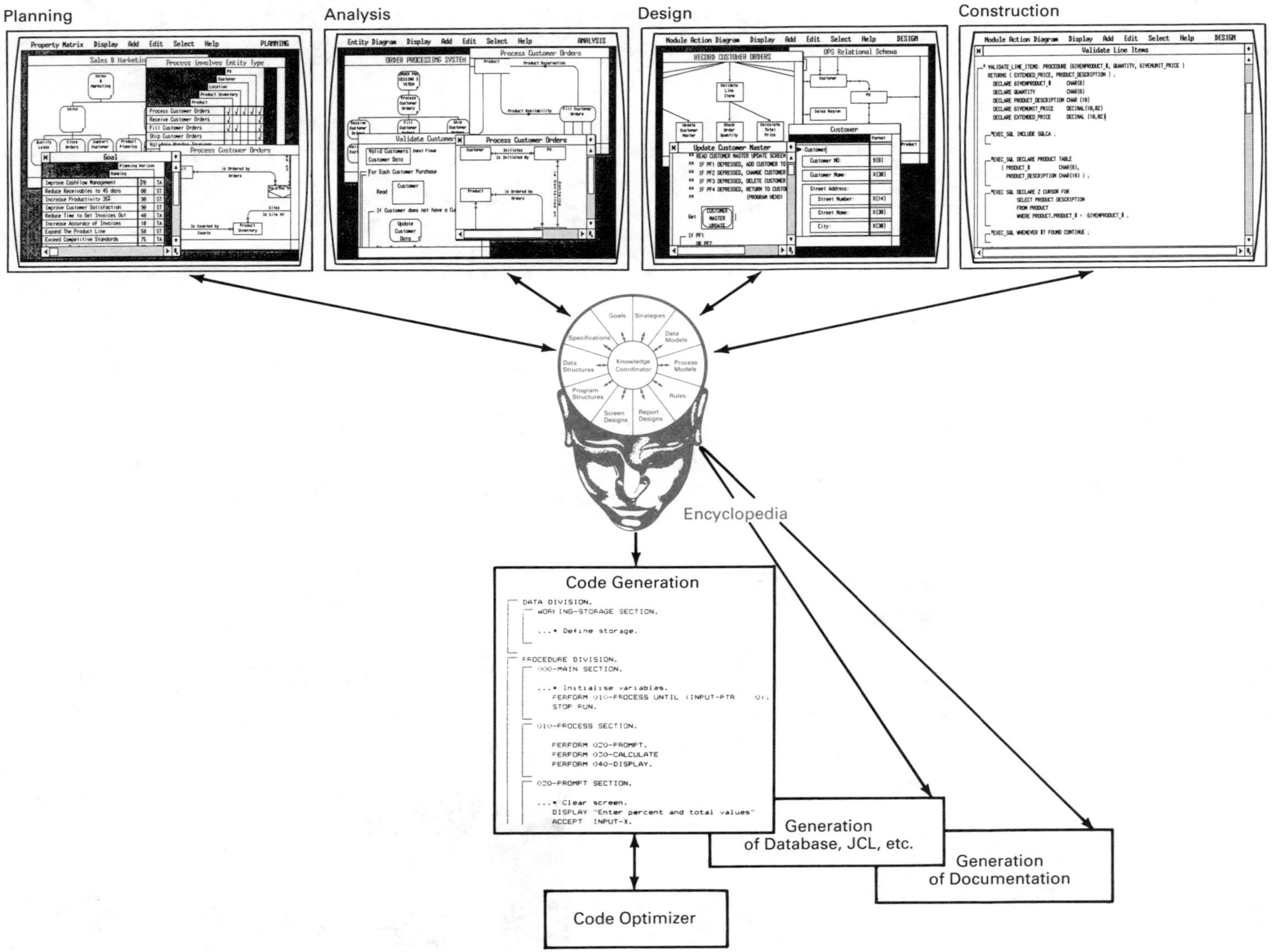

Figure 2.15 An integrated CASE (I-CASE) toolset needs to link the above facilities with com-

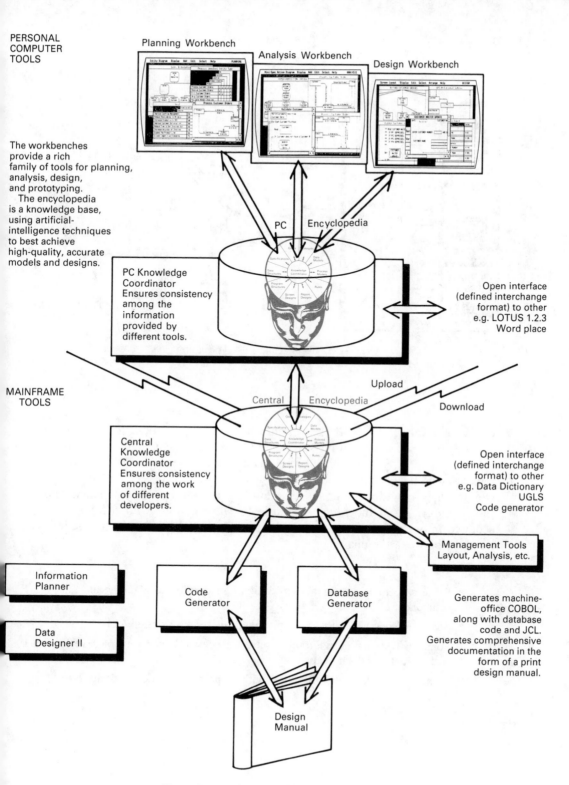

PERSONAL
COMPUTER
TOOLS

Planning Workbench

Analysis Workbench

Design Workbench

The workbenches
provide a rich
family of tools for planning,
analysis, design,
and prototyping.
   The encyclopedia
is a knowledge base,
using artificial-
intelligence techniques
to best achieve
high-quality, accurate
models and designs.

PC   Encyclopedia

PC Knowledge
Coordinator
Ensures consistency
among the
information
provided by
different tools.

Open interface
(defined interchange
format) to other
e.g. LOTUS 1.2.3
Word place

MAINFRAME
TOOLS

Central   Encyclopedia

Upload

Download

Central
Knowledge
Coordinator
Ensures consistency
among the work
of different
developers.

Open interface
(defined interchange
format) to other
e.g. Data Dictionary
UGLS
Code generator

Management Tools
Layout, Analysis, etc.

Information
Planner

Code
Generator

Database
Generator

Generates machine-
office COBOL,
along with database
code and JCL.
Generates comprehensive
documentation in the
form of a print
design manual.

Data
Designer II

Design
Manual

Figure 2.16   The KnowledgeWare toolset

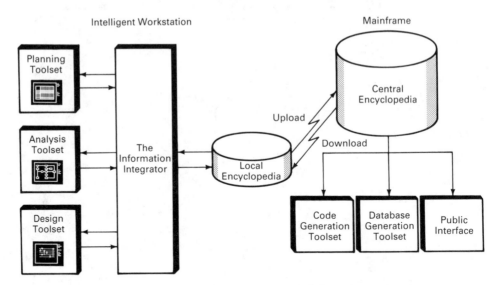

Figure 2.17   The Texas Instruments toolset for information engineering.

**CATEGORIES
OF CASE TOOLS**   It is desirable to have CASE tools for each of the four stages of I.S. development: *planning, analysis, design,* and *construction.* Some organizations sell separate workbenches for each of these sets of activities. It is desirable that such workbenches be fully integrated and employ a common encyclopedia. Work should evolve from the *planning* phase to *construction,* with the knowledge acquired in one phase being used in the next phase. There should be a seamless interface between the phases.

- Some case tools are for system design and contain no planning and analysis components.
- Some are code generators with planning, analysis, or design tools.
- Some analysis and design toolkits have a process-oriented view of development with no data modeling capability.
- Some provide data modeling tools without process analysis or design.

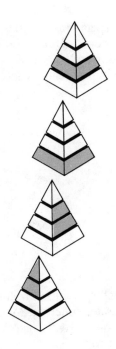

An *I-CASE* environment provides an *integrated* set of tools for *all* parts of the pyramid.

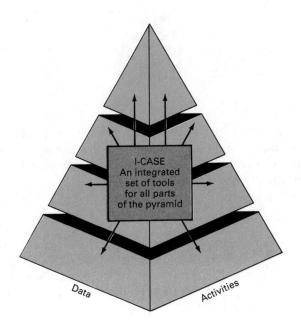

Some corporations have specialized in building code generators without front-end design and analysis tools. Other corporations have built planning, analysis, and design tools without a back-end code generator. Many attempts have been made to couple front-end analysis loosely and design tools to back-end code generators.

This is not a fully satisfactory solution because much manual work is still needed to make the code generator function. What is needed is full integration between the CASE front-end tools and the generator so that code is automatically generated from the front-end tools.

The term I-CASE should be used only to relate to products with this full integration. This implies that the front-end tools and the code generators use the same encyclopedia. The encyclopedia should generate program code, database code, and documentation, as illustrated in Fig. 2.15.

SUMMARY
OF TOOL
CHARACTERISTICS

Box 2.1 summarizes characteristics of CASE tools. Box 2.2 summarizes characteristics of I-CASE tools. The features above are basic characteristics of CASE tools. A tool should not be referred to as "CASE" if it lacks any of these features.

BOX 2.1 Basic characteristics of CASE tools

CASE software should perform the following functions:

- Enable the user to draw diagrams for planning, analysis, or design on a workstation screen
- Solicit information about the objects in the diagram and relationships among the objects so that a complete set of information is built up
- Store the meaning of the diagram, rather than the diagram itself, in a repository
- Check the diagram for accuracy, integrity, and completeness. The diagram types used should be chosen to facilitate this
- Enable the user to employ multiple types of diagrams representing different facets of an analysis or design
- Enable the user to draw programs with diagrams, showing conditions, loops, CASE structures, and other constructs of structural programming
- Enforce structured modeling and design of a type that enables accuracy and consistency checks to be as complete as possible
- Coordinate the information on multiple diagrams, checking that they are consistent, and *together* have accuracy, integrity, and completeness
- Store the information built up at workstations in a central repository shared by all analysts and designers
- Coordinate the information in the central repository, ensuring consistency among the work of all analysts and designers

BOX 2.2 Basic characteristics of I-CASE tools. (An extension of the characteristics in Box 2.1.)

- The activities of planning, analysis, design, and construction each have a software workbench with multiple tools. These workbenches are fully integrated so that one workbench directly employs the information from another.
- An encyclopedia stores the knowledge from the multiple workbenches in an integrated manner.
- A code generator is fully integrated with the design workbench (as opposed to having a bridge to a separate code generator with its own separate syntax).
- The generator employs the facilities of requisite operating systems and database management systems, including the data dictionary.
- The generator generates the requisite database statements and job control language.
- The output of the generator may be fed into an optimizer, which adjusts the code and database accesses to give optimal machine performance.
- The tools support all phases of the project life cycle in an integrated manner.
- In addition to supporting project life cycles, an I-CASE toolkit supports enterprise-wide planning, data modeling, and process modeling to create a framework into which many project life cycles fit. In other words, the toolkit is designed for information engineering rather than merely software engineering.
- System design employs entity-relationship models and data models with full normalization.
- The planning, analysis, and design workbenches can support user workshops such as JRP (joint requirements planning) and JAD (joint application design).
- The design workbench employs a screen designer, dialog designer, and report designer, each of which is integrated with the encyclopedia.
- Code structures are represented graphically (by action diagrams or similar diagrams).
- Thorough documentation is generated automatically.
- The toolkit enables highly complex systems to be subdivided into less complex systems that can be developed by separate small teams. The interface between the separate systems is defined with precision in the encyclopedia.
- The toolkit incorporates the characteristics of CASE tools listed in Box 2.1.

REFERENCES

1. For updated reviews and evaluations of significant CASE and I-CASE products, refer to *Computer-Aided Software Engineering,* Volume 6, of The James Martin Productivity Series, published by High-Productivity Software Inc., 36 Bessom Street, Marblehead, MA 01945 (617-639-1958 or 800-242-1240).

2. Diagramming standards are described in James Martin, *Recommended Diagramming Standards for Computing,* Prentice-Hall, Inc., Englewood Cliffs, NJ, 1986, and more briefly in Book II of this trilogy.

3 THE ROLE OF DATA MODELS

INTRODUCTION
INTRODUCTION The basic premise of information engineering is that data lie at the center of modern data processing. This is illustrated in Fig. 3.1. The data are stored and maintained with the aid of various types of data systems software. The processes on the left in Fig. 3.1 *create* and *modify* the data. The data must be captured and entered with appropriate accuracy controls. The data will be updated periodically. The processes on the right of Fig. 3.1 use the data. Routine documents such as invoices, receipts, freight bills, and work tickets are printed. Executives or professionals sometimes search for information. They create summaries or analyses of the data, and produce charts and reports. They ask "What-if?" questions and use the data to help them make decisions. Auditors check the data and attempt to ensure that data are not misused.

The data in Fig. 3.1 may be in multiple data systems. They may be stored in different ways. They will often be distributed. They are often updated and used by means of transmission links and personal computers.

A second basic premise of information engineering is that the *types* of data used in an enterprise do not change very much. The entity types do not change, except for the occasional (rare) addition of new entity types. The types of *attributes* that we store about these entities also change infrequently. The *values* of data change constantly, like the data in a flight information board at an airport, but the *structure* of the data, like the board itself, does not change much if it was well designed to begin with.

DATA ADMINISTRATION Given a certain collection of data item types there is a correct way to represent them. The *data administrator* uses formal techniques (which have been automated) to create stable models of the data. He creates an entity-relationship

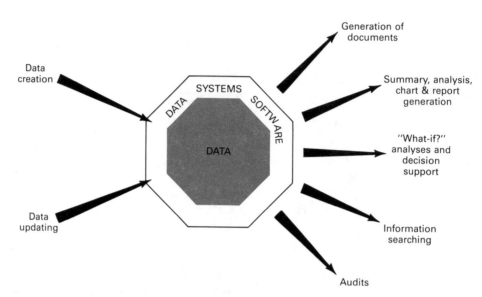

Figure 3.1 Most modern data processing is composed of actions that create and modify data, with appropriate accuracy controls, and processes that use, analyze, summarize, and manipulate data, or print documents from the data.

model with data that is correctly normalized. This is discussed in Book II of this trilogy. If well designed, these models change little and we can usually avoid changes that are disruptive. In information engineering these models become a foundation stone on which most computerized procedures are built.

Although the data is relatively stable, the procedures that use the data change fast and frequently. In fact, it is desirable that systems analysts and end users should be able to change them frequently. We need maximum flexibility in improving administrative procedures and adapting them to the rapidly changing needs of management. Every business changes dynamically and the views of management on how to run it change much faster.

While procedures change rapidly (or should), and the computer programs, processes, networks, and hardware change, but the basic types of data are relatively stable. The foundation stone of data is feasible only if the data is identified and structured correctly so that it can be used with the necessary flexibility.

Because the basic data types are stable whereas procedures tend to change, *data-oriented* techniques if correctly applied, succeed where *procedure-oriented* techniques have failed. Many of the procedure-oriented techniques have resulted in systems that are slow to implement and difficult to change. Information engineering seeks to fulfill management's changing needs rapidly and obtain results quickly, once the necessary data infrastructure is established, by using high-level database languages and application generators.

In the 1970s the practice of *data administration* grew up. Some enterprises learned how to do data administration effectively. They appointed a data administrator at a high level in the I.S. organization. His job was to:

- Identify the types of data used in an enterprise
- Obtain agreement about their names and definitions
- Obtain agreement about how they were represented in computers
- Design an entity-relationship model with fully normalized data for all (or most) of the data in the enterprise
- Represent the data model in a data dictionary
- Ensure that system builders conform to the data models as far as possible
- Resolve conflicts about incompatible representations of data
- Advise in the selection of database management systems, a goal being to achieve data independence in programs
- Advise in the design of databases that used the data model
- Advise in the selection of database languages, including end-user languages

By the 1980s there was much experience of data administration. Books were written on how to succeed in doing it as effectively as possible [1]. It became clear that data administration needed to be part of the broader framework of information engineering. In some corporations the data administrator was promoted to become chief information engineer. Only about a third of large corporations succeeded in doing data administration well. These corporations were generally the first to reap the benefits of information engineering.

The term *information engineering* is sometimes contrasted with the term *software engineering*. The primary focus of software engineering is the logic that is used in computerized processes: Specifications and programs must be structured correctly. The primary focus of data administration is that the data should be correctly structured: The "logical" representation of data should be fully normalized and independent of specific programs that use the data because many different programs must share the data.

Software engineering techniques became formalized in the 1970s. They encompass software development methodologies such as structured programming, structured design, and structured analysis, and tools to support these. They are vital in the creation of complex software with complex logic. Measurements of programmers' productivity, error rates, and, particularly, maintenance costs demonstrated that *fully structured programming is far more cost-effective than semistructured programming,* which many programmers practice under the name of *structured programming*. Fully structured programming can be enforced with the right computerized tools.

Data modeling techniques also became formalized in the 1970s. Data models can be designed with a formal technique and are independent of the logic of the applications that use the model. *The data model, if correctly designed, is likely to be stable even though the procedures that use the model change frequently.* Computerized tools can help in the correct normalization of data (as discussed in Book II of this trilogy).

Software engineering often advocated a *process-centered* view of development in which the design of data was an adjunct to the design of procedures. Information engineering advocates a *data-centered* view of development in which the logical design of normalized data is done centrally by a data administrator. In practice, formally structured data models and formally structured design of procedures need to interlink. Both should be built with computerized tools that help to achieve the correct structures. The formal design of procedures is tightly linked to the formal data models.

PROBLEMS WITH DATA DESIGNED APPLICATION BY APPLICATION

Traditionally, each functional area in an organization has developed its own files and procedures. There has been much redundancy in data. A medium-sized firm might have many departments, each doing its own purchasing, for example. Before computers, this redundancy did not matter; it was probably the best way to operate. After computers, however, it did matter. There might be a dozen sets of purchasing programs to be maintained instead of one. There might be a dozen sets of incompatible purchasing files. The incompatibility prevented overall management information from being pulled together.

Earlier, data processing installations implemented applications independently from one another. (Many still do.) Integrating the different applications seemed too difficult. Integration grew slowly *within* departments or functional areas. To achieve integration *among* functional areas would have required new types of management.

Each functional area had its own procedures, which it understood very well. It did not understand the procedures of other areas. Each area kept its own files. The structure of these files was unique to the responsibilities of that area. Unfortunately, data had to pass among the areas, and management data had to be extracted from multiple areas. This data was usually incompatible. Worse, individual areas frequently found the need to change their data structures, and often did so without appreciating the chain reaction of problems caused by the change. Figure 3.2 shows the environment of this data processing style.

When each functional area has its own files and procedures there is a complex flow of paperwork between the areas to reflect changes in all versions of the data. When this is computerized with separate files, the system is complex and inflexible. Data for different areas is separately designed and not equivalent. Accuracy is lost. Items "slip through the cracks" in the paperwork processes. Maintenance and change are difficult to accomplish, so the procedures become rigid. Management information spanning the areas cannot be extracted.

In this nonintegrated environment, most communication of changes is done by paperwork, which is error prone, time consuming, and highly labor intensive. Suppose, for example, that Engineering prepares an engineering change report and makes multiple copies: one for Production Control, one for Inventory Control, one for Accounting, and so on. Production Control concludes that the engineering change requires changes to the product file. It requires a new request for materials to be sent to Inventory Control. Inventory Control must determine the effects of the change on purchasing operations. These affect the costs of raw materials and parts. Inventory Control communicates these to Accounting. Accounting concludes that a change in sales price is necessary to retain profitability and communicates this need to Marketing. And so on.

When data for different areas is separately defined and incompatible, this passing of information among the separate systems is complex and inflexible. Manual handling of paperwork is needed. Accuracy is lost. Items slip through the cracks. Changes made to one system can play havoc with others. To prevent harmful effects of change, the management procedures become rigid and change is made difficult.

In one factory, more than $1 million worth of work-in-progress was unaccounted for on the shop floor due to items "slipping through the cracks" in the paperwork process. This unaccountability was a major motivation for the end-user management to create an integrated on-line system, which totally changed the administrative procedures of the factory.

The solution to the problems illustrated by Fig. 3.2 is centralized planning of the data. It is the job of the data administrator to create a *model* of the data needed to run an organization. This model spans the functional areas. When it is modularized it is broken up by data subjects *rather than by departmental or organization-chart boundaries*. Figure 3.3 illustrates the use of a common data model.

When data is consolidated in database systems, data modeling is the key to success. The data structures become more complex, but the data flows are greatly simplified. The data are consistent and accurate. New forms of management information can be extracted quickly with end-user languages. Changes in procedures can be made rapidly with these languages. Paperwork is greatly lessened. The administrative procedures of the organization need to be completely rethought. Fundamentally different analysis and design techniques are needed.

Information engineering builds up a common data model in the encyclopedia and analyzes the fundamental processes of the enterprise, independently from current systems and procedures. During business area analysis, the model of processes is tightly linked to the normalized data model. This is performed at the screen of the workbench facility (Fig. 3.4). Once the data and fundamental processes of an enterprise have been clearly modeled, the systems and procedures can be streamlined to give the most efficient operation.

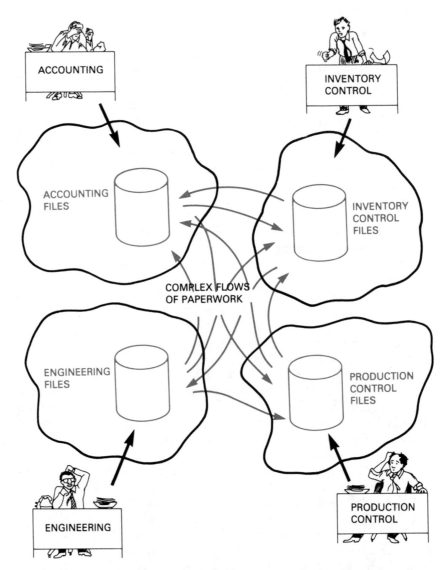

ACCOUNTING

INVENTORY
CONTROL

ACCOUNTING
FILES

INVENTORY
CONTROL
FILES

COMRLEX FLOWS
OF PAPERWORK

ENGINEERING
FILES

PRODUCTION
CONTROL
FILES

ENGINEERING

PRODUCTION
CONTROL

Figure 3.2   Traditionally, each functional area has its own files and procedures. Because of this, there is a complex flow of paperwork between the
areas to reflect changes in all versions of the data. When this is computerized
with separate files, the system is complex and inflexible. Data for different
areas is separately designed and not equivalent. Accuracy is lost. Items "slip
through the cracks" in the paperwork processes. Maintenance and change are
difficult to accomplish, so the procedures become rigid. Management information spanning the areas cannot be extracted.

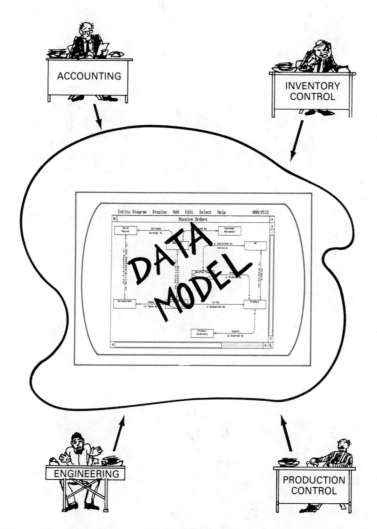

Figure 3.3 When data is consolidated into an integrated database, data modeling is the key to success. The data structures become more complex, but the data flows are greatly simplified. The data is consistent and accurate. New forms of management information can be extracted quickly with fourth-generation languages. Changes in procedures can be made rapidly with these languages. Paperwork is greatly lessened. The administrative procedures of the organization need to be rethought completely. Fundamentally different analysis and design techniques are needed.

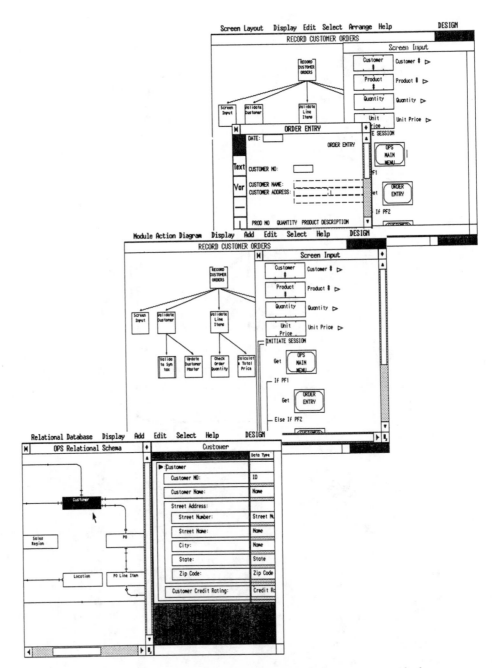

Figure 3.4 The various Information Engineering design screens must be logically linked to the data model that is used.

STABLE FOUNDATION STONE

An entity is anything about which data can be stored: a product, a customer, a salesperson, a part. We draw entities as square-cornered boxes. A data model shows the relationships between entities. These are drawn as lines connecting the boxes. Figure 3.5 shows a simple entity-relationship model. The links are labeled with the name of the relationship. For example, Fig. 3.5 indicates that a CUSTOMER places CUSTOMER-ORDERS, a CUSTOMER-ORDER consists of ORDER-LINES, a PRODUCT is ordered on an ORDER-LINE or is backordered on a BACKORDER, and so on. Other information may be stored about the relationship. For example, a crow's-foot end on a line indicates a one-to-many relationship. A bar across a line indicates a one-to-one relationship. A circle means zero. The following means that a CUSTOMER can place zero or multiple CUSTOMER ORDERS; a CUSTOMER ORDER relates to one CUSTOMER.

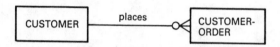

We store *attributes* giving data about the entities. For example, a salesperson has a given address, territory, quota, salary, has sold a certain percentage of his quota, and so on. The data model shows what attributes relate to each entity.

The types of entities and attributes that are used in running a corporation usually remain the same with minor changes. They are the foundation of data processing. Their *values* change constantly. The *information* or types of reports which we extract from that collection of data may change substantially. The information requirements of executives change from month to month. The technology that we use for storing or updating the data will change.

When a corporation changes its administrative procedures, the entities, relationships, and attributes usually remain the same. It may require a small number of new entities or some new attributes for existing entities, so the foundation data model grows somewhat over the years.

A typical medium-sized corporation has several hundred entities (when redundancies are removed). A large diversified corporation has more, and a separate data model might be created for each of its subsidiaries. There are often 10 to 20 attributes for a typical entity.

Many years ago the author worked in a large bank when computers were first introduced. There was batch processing, many manual procedures, no terminals, and much form filling. Today, the customers use automated teller machines on-line to distant computers; there are large numbers of terminals and the administrative procedures have entirely changed. However, the raw types of data that are stored are the same as 20 years earlier. There has been a huge change in automation, but if a data model had been created 20 years ago, it would still be valid today, with minor changes.

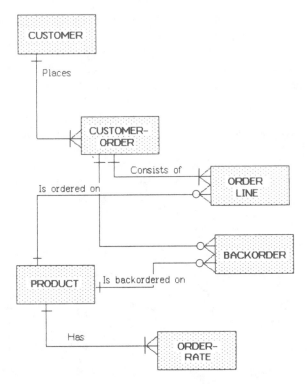

Figure 3.5   Portion of an entity-relationship model.

Of course, if the bank decided to diversify into the whisky distillation business (appropriate for some bankers), a fundamentally different data model would have to be created and added on to the existing model. With some database management software new attributes can be added without causing disruption. New entities can be added. Some types of data system software have more flexibility than others. An appropriate choice is needed.

It might be argued that some enterprises change more than banks in the types of data they use. That is true, so their data models need to be updated, preferably in an automated fashion.

STABLE DATABASES

There is a huge difference between databases which are specifically designed to be stable, and the files that have been used in traditional data processing. Typical file structures tend to change continually because the requirements of users change. No enterprise is static, and management perceptions of what information is needed change rapidly.

Database technology seeks to isolate the programs from the changes in data structures. We use the term *data independence,* which means that when the data structure changes, the programs keep running because they are isolated from that change. The programs have a "view" of the data which can be preserved even though the actual, physical structure of the data changes.

Data independence is achieved by means of database management systems. The most important difference between a database management system and a file management system is that database management translates between the application program's view of data and the actual structure of the data. It preserves the program's view of data when the actual view changes in either a logical or a physical manner. With database systems many application programs can have different views of the same data.

The use of a good database management system does not, by itself, give us the protection we need. We also need good logical design of the data structures used.

LOGICAL DESIGN OF DATABASES

Unless controlled, systems analysts tend to design records that group together any collection of data items which they perceive as being useful. All manner of anomalies can arise because of inappropriate grouping of data items. Some of these anomalies are subtle and often not perceived.

A database contains hundreds (and sometimes thousands) of types of data items. If the logical structures are designed badly, a large financial penalty will result. A corporation will not be able to employ the databases as it should, so productivity will suffer. The databases will constantly have to be modified, but they cannot be modified without much application program rewriting. The end users will not be served as they need, and because of this, may try to create their own alternatives to employing the database.

In the late 1970s it became clear that many database installations were not living up to the publicized advantages of database technology. A few rare ones had spectacularly improved the entire data processing function and greatly increased application development speed and productivity. The difference lay in the design of the overall logical structure of the data.

The term *normalized* implies that the data has a correct logical structure representing the inherent properties of the data so that the data can be used for multiple types of applications. Normalization is discussed in Book II. The data on a purchase order, waybill, or other document is not normalized. If the data in a database is not correctly normalized, a new application may not be able to use the data in the database. It would be too expensive to restructure the data because that would require the rewriting of applications that use the data. In this situation a new file may be built for the application. Many new applications have the same problem, so many new files are built and the database concept breaks down. Correctly normalized data, then, are desirable for the concept of shared databases to work.

STEP-BY-STEP BUILDING OF THE MODEL

In the practice of information engineering a high-level overview of the data is created at the top level of the pyramid (Fig. 3.6). This overview is a diagram of the entity types in an enterprise and the relation-

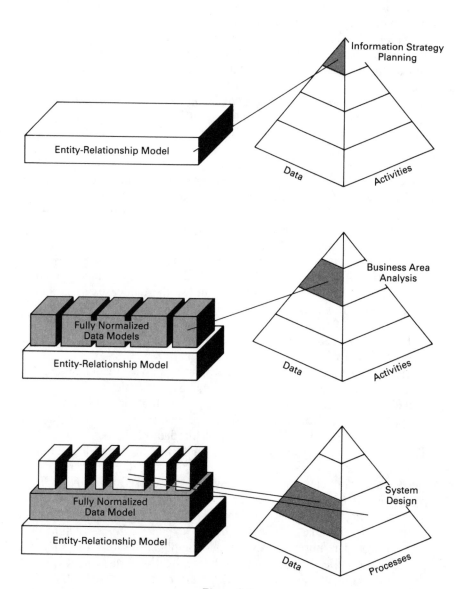

Figure 3.6

ships among them. It is built with a computerized tool so that it can be added to constantly and so that a computer can reorganize the diagram. At this initial stage there is no attempt to identify attributes, to normalize the data, or to detect the subtle variations in entities or intersections (discussed in Book II). The initial requirement is an overview of the data across the entire enterprise (or the portion of it selected for study).

At the second level of the pyramid, details of attributes are added and a normalized data model is built (Fig. 3.6). This model is usually created for one business area at a time. It is part of the work of business area analysis—stage 2 of information engineering. It is a process of adding more detail to the overview model built in stage 1. When an entity is examined at this stage it may already have been modeled in detail in a different business area. The encyclopedia makes this known. There may be some resolution needed of conflicting representations of attributes. It is the task of the data administrator to resolve such conflicts. There are likely to be certain data for which conflicting definitions remain. A large enterprise rarely achieves perfection in data modeling. The encyclopedia needs to be able to handle conflicting definitions where they occur.

Many corporations have normalized data models. For many years, preparing these models has been the task of data administrators. Corporations with data models are now linking them into the broader scope of information engineering.

USING THE DATA MODEL

System design proceeds by using the data in the data model (the bottom of Fig. 3.6). The tools for computer aided system design must link tightly to the computerized representation of the data model. From an overall logical model of the data in an enterprise, submodels are extracted for the design of specific systems. During the design phase, the data structure is adapted to the capabilities of a specific database or file management system.

In certain cases the data structures used in working systems deviate from the logical data model. The data may be denormalized in some way to achieve greater machine performance. Designers need to think through the possible adverse consequences of this.

THE BUILDING BLOCKS OF INFORMATION ENGINEERING

Information engineering provides an integrated set of methodologies as shown in Fig. 3.7. In this diagram each block is dependent on the one beneath it. However, the blocks can be assembled in different ways.

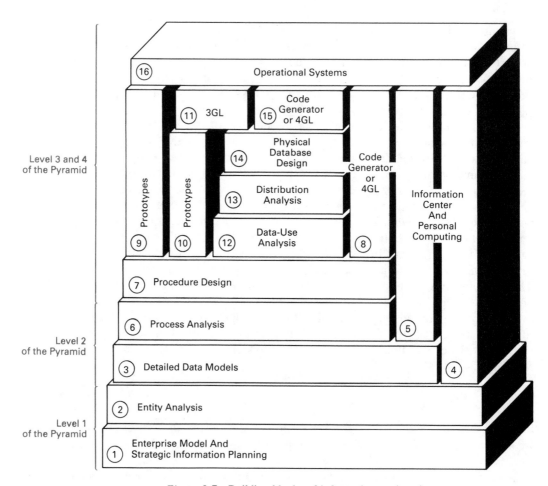

Figure 3.7 Building blocks of information engineering.

Block 1

The block on which all the others rest relates to strategic planning. A hierarchical model of the enterprise is drawn, the objectives of the enterprise and its components are established, and attempts are made to determine what information is needed to enable the enterprise to accomplish its objectives.

Block 2

The next block creates an overview map of the data needed to run the enterprise. This is a top-down analysis of the types of data that must be kept and how they relate to one another. Information analysis is sometimes done across an entire enterprise; sometimes it is done for one division, subsidiary, factory, or portion of an enterprise.

Block 3

The third block is *data modeling*. Information analysis surveys the types of data needed. It creates an information model, which is a broad overview but does not contain all the details needed for database implementation. Data modeling creates the detailed logical database design and attempts to make it as stable as possible before it is implemented. Block 3 is an extension of block 2 that carries it into more detail, normalizes the data, and applies various checks for stability.

Blocks 4 and 5

Many new languages and generators are employable by end users. This direct involvement of end users can bring a vitally needed improvement in the I.S. process, provided that the users do not invent their own data structures. In many cases, users do exactly that, glad of their newfound liberation from the I.S. programming organization. Where the data is shared data, rather than personal data, the use of end-user languages should be linked into the data models as represented by blocks 4 and 5 in Fig. 3.7.

In some cases, personal computing and information-center computing employ data that is not fully normalized and not represented in the detailed data models. For this reason, block 4 of Fig. 3.7 rests on block 2. On the other hand, where the data needed is in the data administrator's detailed models, the users should employ them. This will save them from having to design their own data, which takes time, and will help to ensure the exchange of data among separately developed systems. Where possible, then, end-user-oriented computing should, like block 5, rest on block 3.

Block 6

Block 6 refers to the analysis of a specific business area. The functions of the area are decomposed into *processes,* using decomposition diagrams. Dependency diagrams or data-flow diagrams may be drawn, showing the interrelations among processes.

In some cases, process analysis is tightly linked to the creation of data models. While the processes are being examined, the entity types needed are considered. The data items needed may be determined and synthesized into a fully normalized data model. If a data model already exists, this will serve to check its accuracy and completeness. A matrix may be developed that shows which processes use which entity types and how they use them.

Block 7

Block 7 is concerned with the design of procedures. The design of a procedure often uses multiple types of diagrams tightly linked via the encyclopedia. A subset of the overall data model is extracted from the encyclopedia along with

any other information that helps in the design. The diagrams created are linked
to this data submodel.

To speed up the work of the designer, automated graphics tools enable
these types of diagrams to be drawn, organized, and changed quickly. The tools
should enforce rigor in the drawing; automatically convert the various representations into action diagrams (Book III of this trilogy); facilitate the cutting, pasting, and editing of action diagrams; and help convert the action diagrams to
code. The use of action diagrams permits the design to be taken as far as possible before committing to a specific language and makes it as easy as possible
to switch from one language to another.

Blocks 8 and 9

The design created in block 7 may be implemented directly with a code generator or with a fourth-generation language such as FOCUS, RAMIS II, IDEAL,
Application Factory, NATURAL II, or MANTIS [2]. Alternatively, such languages or generators may be used to create a *prototype*. The prototype may be
successively modified and may eventually become the operational code.

Blocks 10 and 11

In other cases, the prototype may have insufficient machine performance to be
the final system. The prototype may be converted to COBOL or some other
lower-level language that can be better optimized for performance.

Block 12

Data use analysis (block 12 of Fig. 3.7) provides a formal way of collecting
and diagramming the usage information ready for physical database design
(block 14). Data modeling results in a logical design of a database. A variety
of decisions have to be made before that design is implemented physically. The
decisions depend on how the data is likely to be used, the usage paths through
the database, and their volumes of use and response-time needs. This information is gathered in the stage of block 12.

Block 13

There are many reasons for distributing systems and many different forms of
distribution. Data models may be split for implementation in separate databases.
Block 13 relates to distribution analysis.

Block 14

Block 14 relates to the conversion of the data models and procedures into physical database design. Some database management systems make it advantageous

to deviate from clearly structured fully normalized data for certain systems where heavy-duty computing makes performance considerations paramount.

Block 15

Implementation may be done with code generators or 4GLs (block 15) or third-generation languages such as COBOL (block 11). The key to achieving much higher productivity in I.S. is to couple the design-automation tools of information engineering to code generators.

Block 16

When the system is operational, maintenance is an ongoing concern. Maintenance should be done, not by changing COBOL programs, but by changing the diagrams and regenerating wherever possible.

THE DATA ADMINISTRATOR

Data modeling plays a vital part in the building blocks of Fig. 3.7. Many corporations now have well-established techniques for doing it as effectively as possible [1]. It is important to distinguish clearly between a data administrator and a database designer. The *database designer* is a technician concerned with a specific database. He designs its physical structure to be as effective and machine efficient as possible. This task may be associated with a given project. The *data administrator,* on the other hand, has a high-level job of planning, modeling, and coordinating the corporation's data. This is not a job requiring technical skills, but a task of understanding the data needed to run the business and making diverse individuals agree about the definition and representation of data items. Many different views of data are synthesized with the aid of a computerized tool into a fully normalized data model.

Although some corporations have done an excellent job of data modeling and data administration, others have disastrously failed to achieve any overall coordination of data. This failure is extremely expensive in the long run in inflated I.S. costs, failure to implement needed procedures, and in lost business.

Many corporations have not made a serious attempt at data administration and allow systems to be built with ad hoc file design. Some corporations have tried to achieve data administration and failed. The reasons for the failure are listed in Box 3.1. Box 3.2 lists the human and technical requirements needed for success.

In many organizations the lack of good database design and integration results in huge maintenance costs and delays. Procedures cannot be changed quickly. New procedures that are urgently needed take years to introduce.

When independent system builders are hard at work, without coordination in many cases, they do an excellent job. However, the types of data they use overlap substantially, and this is often not recognized. Their systems need to be

BOX 3.1 Reasons for failure of corporate data administration

Many early attempts at corporate data administration failed. The reasons for failure were as follows:

- Organizational politics prevailed, because of a lack of strong management and direction from the top.
- The human problems of making different accounts or managers agree on the definitions of data items were not dealt with.
- The magnitude of the task was underestimated.
- The data administrator was a low-paid technician.
- Methodologies for the design of stable data structures were not understood.
- The necessary data models were too complex to design and administer by hand, and appropriate computerized tools were not used.
- There was not an overall architect who could use the design methodology.
- Attempts of data modeling took too long and users could not wait.
- Data model design was confused with *implementation* and physical database design.

Many corporations have achieved successful administration. Box 3.2 lists the requirements necessary for this to succeed.

BOX 3.2 Essentials for the overall control of data in an enterprise

Human

- Top management must understand the need for information engineering.
- Information that is strategic to the running of the enterprise should be identified (Book II of this trilogy).
- The data administrator must report at a suitably high level and be given full senior management support.

BOX 3.2   *(Continued)*

- The span of control of the data administrator needs to be selected with an understanding of what is politically pragmatic.
- The data administrator must be highly competent at using the design methodology, and the methodology must be automated.
- An appropriate budget for data modeling must be set.
- Data modeling should be quite separate from physical database design.
- End-user teams should be established to assist in data modeling and to review and refine the data models thoroughly.

Technical

- Strategic planning should be done of the entities in an enterprise. All entities should be represented in a rough entity model.
- The rough entity model should be expanded into detailed data models in stages, as appropriate.
- The detailed data model should represent all functional dependencies among the data items.
- All logical data groups should be fully normalized.
- Stability analysis should be applied to the detailed data model.
- The entity model and detailed model should be designed with an automated tool.
- Defined operations may be associated with the data to ensure that integrity, accuracy, and security checks are applied to the data, independent of applications.
- Submodels should be extractable from the overall computerized model when needed for specific projects.
- Ideally, the data modeling tool should provide *automatic* input to the library of the specification language, application generator, or programming language that is used.

connected but often this cannot be done without conversion. Conversion, when the need for it becomes apparent, is often too expensive to accomplish, so incompatible systems live on, making it difficult or impossible to integrate the data that management need. When good database administration has not been done, there can be very expensive surprises late in the development phases or during subsequent evolution.

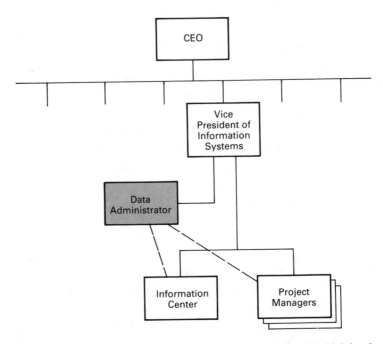

Figure 3.8 The data administrator needs to report at a suitably high level.

**REPORTING AT A
HIGH LEVEL**
The data administrator needs to report at a suitably high level and to have enough "clout" to ensure that good data models are built and adhered to. Effective data administrators often report to the chief MIS executive as shown in Fig. 3.8, with a matrix management link to information centers and project managers.

Information engineering is a substantial step beyond conventional data administration. It requires an administrator of both the data and the other knowledge that resides in the encyclopedia. This person also needs to report at a suitably high level, as discussed in Chapter 4.

REFERENCE

1. James Martin, *Managing the Data-Base Environment,* Prentice-Hall, Inc., Englewood Cliffs, NJ, 1983.

2. James Martin, *Fourth Generation Languages*, Prentice-Hall, Inc., Englewood Cliffs, NJ, 1985.

4 COORDINATION OF ANALYSIS AND DESIGN

INTRODUCTION   A reason why programming, especially the maintenance of programs, is difficult is that the workings of programs are not visible. Complex mechanisms exist but we cannot see them. An important aspect of information engineering, and design automation in general, is that computerized diagrams are used to design programs and systems and to show their inner workings. Most people can understand and modify complex mechanisms much easier when they can see them.

Over the years there have been many different attempts to design programs diagrammatically and to use graphics editors for programming. The types of diagrams used have steadily improved as different structured techniques evolved. However, no single graphic technique has been entirely satisfactory by itself. The reason is that program design is sufficiently complex that *more than one type of diagram is needed*. A designer needs to visualize different aspects of his design in different ways.

A broad overview of a complex system can be visualized with tree-structured diagrams decomposing its functions. An action diagram is probably the best way to represent the overall structure of the programs [1]. The program employs a data model that should be represented graphically [2]. The flow of data or control among the modules of the program may be represented by means of a data-flow diagram or dependency diagram [2]. In special cases other types of diagrams are useful, such as decision trees and tables and finite-state diagrams [3].

The information on the diagrams needs to be interlinked. Most of the diagrams refer to data that is in the data model. The action diagrams can be summarized in a decomposition diagram. The decomposition diagram contains blocks of functionality which are in data flow or dependency diagrams. The relationship between functions and data may be shown in a matrix. And so on.

The diagrams, if they correctly represent a well-designed program or system, are different facets of a single design.

We cannot interlink such diagrams conveniently on a piece of paper. However, *they can be linked with precision when a computerized diagramming tool is used*. The early attempts at building diagramming tools for programmers used only one type of diagram. The tools needed for information engineering represent multiple types of diagrams, each of which is a different facet of the same design. The overall information about the design resides in the encyclopedia. Diagrams are generated from the encyclopedia and may be displayed in multiple windows on a workstation screen. The design may be changed by changing the diagrams. When one diagram is changed, others should automatically change in a corresponding fashion.

As discussed in Chapter 2, the term *hyperdiagram* is used for computerized representations in which multiple diagrams are logically linked together. The hyperdiagram can be explored with windows on the screen of a workbench.

PERSPECTIVES   A common term in database technology is *view*. A view of a database is a representation of data that is perceived by one person or program. The structure of the database may be far more complex than the structure of the view. The view shows only those fields in which the user is interested at this time. The view is a subset of the overall database structure.

A CASE encyclopedia contains many objects and associations among objects. A workstation normally displays some of those objects and associations at one time. It displays a *view* from the encyclopedia contents. An analyst or designer creates a view when he works at the screen. When this view is checked into the central encyclopedia, it becomes part of a much larger representation. The view may have a name and may be referred to in the encyclopedia index so that it can be quickly retrieved.

The view is a hyperdiagram. It contains information about multiple objects and their associations. It can be represented with multiple logically linked screen displays. This compound view is sometimes referred to as a *perspective*. It might alternatively be called a *hyperview*.

A perspective is often worked on by one designer with graphics on a personal computer. It may be worked on in a meeting using a large screen. There may be multiple designers working together on one perspective, each using a workstation linked to a shared facility.

The perspective employs a mini-encyclopedia. The encyclopedia in a personal computer may, at any one time, contain information about only one perspective. The design that emerges has multiple facets, represented by different diagrams and windows and linked by the mini-encyclopedia (see Fig. 4.1). Figures 4.2 through 4.7 represent pieces of the perspective illustrated in Fig. 4.1.

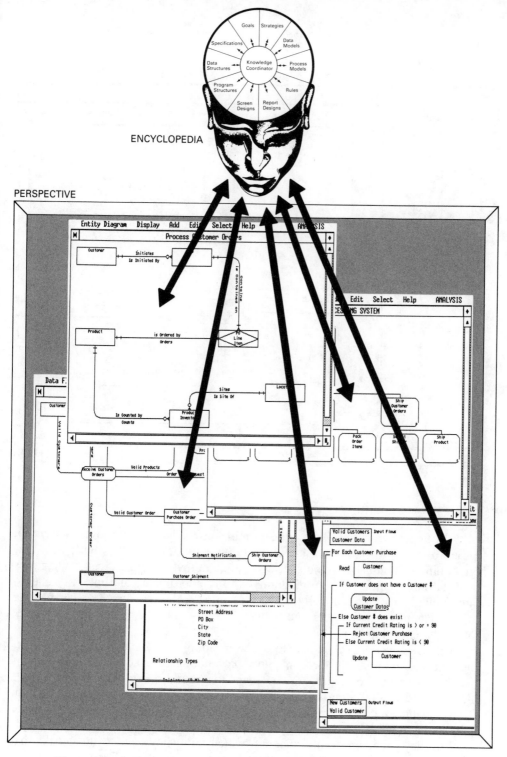

ENCYCLOPEDIA

PERSPECTIVE

Figure 4.1 A *perspective*. Multiple types of diagrams for one design with the knowledge represented on the diagrams tightly linked and cross-checked by the encyclopedia. Figures 4.2 to 4.7 show pieces of the *perspective*.

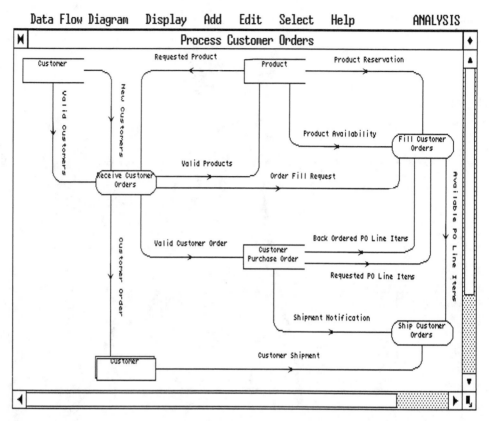

Figure 4.4   A detail window from the perspective illustrated in Figs. 4.1 to 4.7.

A *perspective,* then, is a collection of knowledge about a given activity or group of activities and the data which these activities use. It is built with diagramming techniques and tools. It normally employs multiple types of diagrams and the information in these diagrams is fully coordinated and integrity checks are applied to it automatically. It resides in an encyclopedia. The perspective has an identification number and is one of the formal objects that are kept track of by the encyclopedia.

Because the encyclopedia stores the meaning represented on the diagrams, one type of diagram can be converted into another or used as a component of another diagram. For example, Mr. Jones may build a data-flow diagram (Fig. 4.2). The data-flow diagram shows data stores that can be examined with an entity-relationship diagram (Fig. 4.3). Detail windows may be used to show the data items in entity records (Fig. 4.4). Mr. Smith, working on the same design, may display a decomposition diagram which now shows procedure blocks that Mr. Jones has added to the data-flow diagram (Fig. 4.5). The decomposition

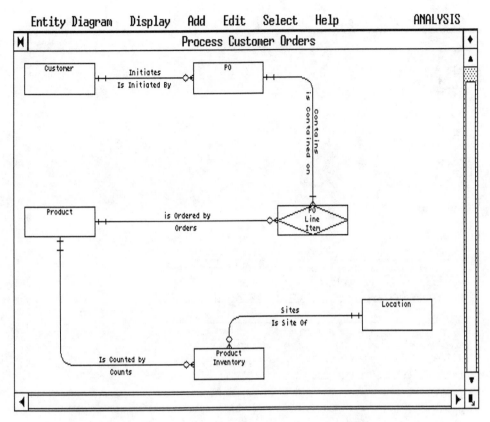

Figure 4.3   Entity-relationship diagram showing the entity-types used in one perspective, and their relationships. This is a subset of a larger data model.

may be shown as an action diagram and program structures developed in the action diagram.

Figure 4.6 shows a data structure diagram with a derived data item OR-DER-DISCOUNT-PERCENTAGE. The derivation of this data item is via a decision tree displayed in a window. Mr. Jones may have built the decision tree. Mr. Smith displays it as an action diagram (Fig. 4.7) and edits it into her overall action diagram, which she then sets to a particular programming language.

Figures 4.2 through 4.7 represent pieces of one perspective. The different diagrams are different facets of the same design, tightly interlinked by the encyclopedia, which stores the meaning of the overall perspective. Particularly important, the diagrams and the perspective as a whole have to conform to rules that check their integrity and consistency. These rules can be applied as the perspective is built, using artificial intelligence techniques. Each diagram type has rules which are applied to it individually, and, in addition, many rules apply to the relationships among diagrams. Several thousand rules have been used for

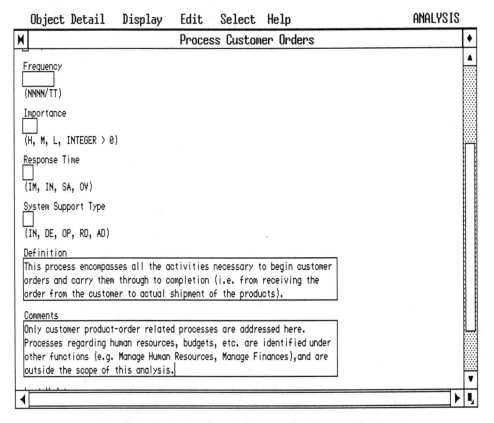

Object Detail   Display   Edit   Select   Help   ANALYSIS

| Process Customer Orders |

Frequency

(NNNN/TT)

Importance

(H, M, L, INTEGER > 0)

Response Time

(IM, IN, SA, OV)

System Support Type

(IN, DE, OP, RD, AD)

Definition
This process encompasses all the activities necessary to begin customer orders and carry them through to completion (i.e. from receiving the order from the customer to actual shipment of the products).

Comments
Only customer product-order related processes are addressed here. Processes regarding human resources, budgets, etc. are identified under other functions (e.g. Manage Human Resources, Manage Finances),and are outside the scope of this analysis.

Figure 4.4   A detail window from the perspective illustrated in Figs. 4.1 to 4.7.

checking the integrity and consistency of perspectives [4]. There is thus high precision and tight control in the relationships between the facets of a perspective.

The example above was one of system design. Perspectives also apply to the other levels of the pyramid. For example, at level 2 an analyst creates a data model with entity-relationship diagrams and details of logical records, process dependency or flow diagrams, process decompositions, and a matrix showing what processes use what entity types.

At the top level an organization chart and a function decomposition chart are used. Matrices map the organization unit to goals and critical success factors. These may be mapped to problems and information needs for overcoming problems, and so on. There are multiple relationships among different objects described in information planning (discussed in Book II). Figure 4.8 shows the types of diagrams that may be used at different levels of the pyramid, and interlinked, where appropriate, into perspectives.

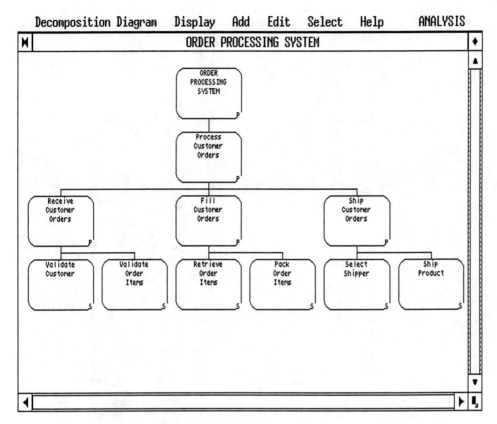

Figure 4.5 A decomposition diagram of the perspective illustrated in Figs. 4.1 to 4.7. The personal computer should coordinate also pieces of the perspective to ensure consistency. A mainframe *knowledge* coordinator should ensure consistency among multiple perspectives.

THE DIAGRAMS ARE THE DOCUMENTATION

The diagrams become the documentation for systems (along with the additional information collected in the encyclopedia when the diagrams were drawn).

When changes are made to systems, the diagrams will be changed on the screen, and the code will be regenerated. The design documentation does not then slip out of date as changes are made.

The computer controls entry of information into the encyclopedia via various diagramming conventions; it analyzes and correlates this information as the knowledgebase grows to increasing levels of detail. The encyclopedia often stores information that is not shown graphically on the diagram. Some of this information may be collected from the analyst or designer when building the diagram at the screen. It is desirable that the user of a graphic workstation be able to display the detailed text or file information. He may do that by pointing

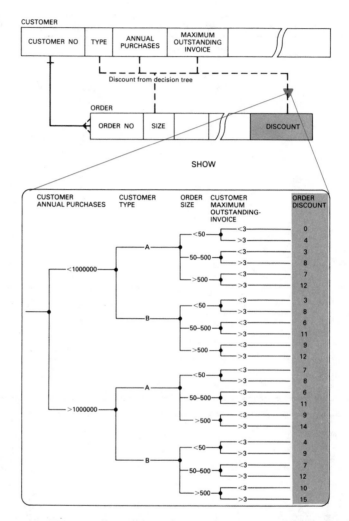

Figure 4.6 The command "SHOW" explodes an icon into a different form
of representation. Here the derivation of a data item is shown as a decision
tree. The converse command is "HIDE." Decision trees can be converted
automatically to action diagrams (Fig. 4.7) showing program code.

to symbols on the diagram and using a command such as DISPLAY or SHOW
AS.

Some analyst workbench tools have been predominantly text oriented, with
diagrams as an insert into the text. This approach copies the style of manual
specifications. It is inappropriate for building today's systems. The workbench
should be oriented around high-precision diagrams with the ability to display
text or data windows to give comments or details not on the diagram. Text,

where it is used, should be a subroutine of the diagrams (displayed with windows) rather than diagrams being a subroutine of the text.

A fundamental principle of information engineering is that the plans, models, specifications, and designs should be computer processable. A computer must "understand" them, apply rules to them, coordinate them in complex ways while catching errors wherever possible, and eventually use them to generate code.

```
IF CUSTOMER.ANNUAL PURCHASES =< 1000000
   IF CUSTOMER.TYPE = A
      IF ORDER.SIZE < 50
         IF CUSTOMER.MAXIMUM_OUTSTANDING_INVOICE =< 3
            ORDER.DISCOUNT = 0
         ELSE
            ORDER.DISCOUNT = 4
         ENDIF
      ELSEIF ORDER.SIZE > 50 AND < 500
         IF CUSTOMER.MAXIMUM_OUTSTANDING_INVOICE =< 3
            ORDER.DISCOUNT = 3
         ELSE
            ORDER.DISCOUNT = 8
         ENDIF
      ELSEIF ORDER.SIZE > 500
         IF CUSTOMER.MAXIMUM_OUTSTANDING_INVOICE =< 3
            ORDER.DISCOUNT = 7
         ELSE
            ORDER.DISCOUNT = 12
         ENDIF
      ENDIF
   ELSEIF CUSTOMER.TYPE = B
      IF ORDER.SIZE < 50
         IF CUSTOMER.MAXIMUM_OUTSTANDING_INVOICE =< 3
            ORDER.DISCOUNT = 3
         ELSE
            ORDER.DISCOUNT = 8
         ENDIF
      ELSEIF ORDER.SIZE > 50 AND < 500
         IF CUSTOMER.MAXIMUM_OUTSTANDING_INVOICE =< 3
            ORDER.DISCOUNT = 6
         ELSE
            ORDER.DISCOUNT = 11
         ENDIF
      ELSEIF ORDER.SIZE > 500
         IF CUSTOMER.MAXIMUM_OUTSTANDING_INVOICE =< 3
            ORDER.DISCOUNT = 9
         ELSE
            ORDER.DISCOUNT = 14
         ENDIF
      ENDIF
   ENDIF
ENDIF
```

Figure 4.7 Action diagram equivalent to the decision tree of Fig. 4.6.

(Continued)

```
ELSE
   IF CUSTOMER.TYPE = A
      IF ORDER.SIZE < 50
         IF CUSTOMER.MAXIMUM_OUTSTANDING_INVOICE = < 3
            ORDER.DISCOUNT = 3
         ELSE
            ORDER.DISCOUNT = 8
         ENDIF
      ELSEIF ORDER.SIZE > 50 AND < 500
         IF CUSTOMER.MAXIMUM_OUTSTANDING_INVOICE =< 3
            ORDER.DISCOUNT = 6
         ELSE
            ORDER.DISCOUNT = 11
         ENDIF
      ELSEIF ORDER.SIZE > 500
         IF CUSTOMER.MAXIMUM_OUTSTANDING_INVOICE =< 3
            ORDER.DISCOUNT = 9
         ELSE
            ORDER.DISCOUNT = 14
         ENDIF
      ENDIF
   ELSEIF CUSTOMER.TYPE = B
      IF ORDER.SIZE < 5-
         IF CUSTOMER.MAXIMUM_OUTSTANDING_INVOICE =< 3
            ORDER.DISCOUNT = 4
         ELSE
            ORDER.DISCOUNT = 9
         ENDIF
      ELSEIF ORDER.SIZE > 50 AND < 500
         IF CUSTOMER.MAXIMUM_OUTSTANDING_INVOICE =< 3
            ORDER.DISCOUNT = 7
         ELSE
            ORDER.DISCOUNT = 12
         ENDIF
      ELSEIF ORDER.SIZE > 500
         IF CUSTOMER.MAXIMUM_OUTSTANDING_INVOICE =< 3
            ORDER.DISCOUNT = 10
         ELSE
            ORDER.DISCOUNT = 15
         ENDIF
      ENDIF
   ENDIF
ENDIF
```

Figure 4.7 (Continued)

It is important to state that a computer cannot understand *text* today. Text is not an appropriate representation for specifications in an automated environment. A more formal computer-processible representation is needed. Diagrams, menus, and fill-in-the-blanks windows give a means of creating specifications that are both computer processible and easy for human beings to understand. Text specifications or comments, where they exist, are for the benefit of people involved with the system.

It is important that everyone understands the principle: *Text is for people. Nontext CASE representations are for computers.* Classical methodologies were

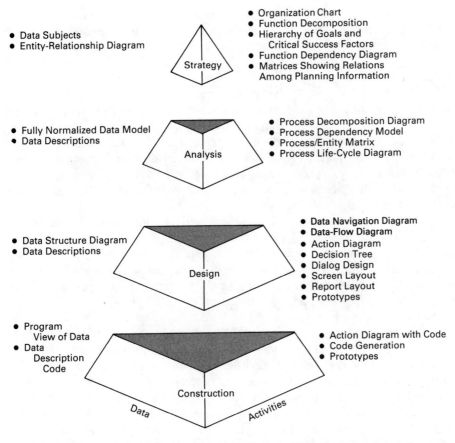

Figure 4.8 The types of diagrams used at each level of information engineering.

mostly text oriented. These need to be replaced by computer-oriented methodologies as quickly as possible.

Some diagramming techniques are more appropriate than others for automation. Automation of diagramming should lead to *automated checking of specifications* and *automatic generation of program code*. Many of the diagramming techniques of the past are not a sound basis for computerized design. They are too casual, unstructured, and cannot represent some of the necessary constructs.

Mathematics is the preeminent language of precision. However, it would be difficult to describe a large road map in mathematics. If we succeeded in doing so, the road map would still be more useful than the mathematics to most people. Data processing is complex and needs road maps. We need to be able to follow the lines, examine the junctions, and read the words on the diagrams.

Some diagrams, however, have a mathematical basis. With mathematics, we may state axioms that the diagrams must obey. A workstation may beep at a designer whenever he violates one of the axioms. The mathematically based structure that emerges may be cross-checked in various ways and may be the basis of automatic generation of code.

THE NEED
FOR FORMALITY

As we commented, architects, surveyors, and persons designing machine parts have *formal* techniques for diagramming which they *must* follow. Systems analysis and program design have even greater need for clear diagrams because these activities are more complex and the work of different people must interlock in intricate ways. There tends, however, to be less formality in programming as yet, perhaps because it is a young discipline full of brilliant people who want to make up their own methods.

One of the reasons why building and maintaining software systems is so expensive and error prone is the difficulty we have in clearly communicating our ideas to one another. Whether we are reading a functional specification, a program design, or a program listing, we often experience difficulty understanding precisely what its author is telling us. Whenever we must rely on our own interpretation of the meaning, the chance of a misunderstanding leading to program errors is very great.

The larger the team, the greater the need for computer-enforced precision. It is difficult or impossible for members of a large team to understand in detail the work of the others. Instead, each team member should be familiar with an overview of the system and see where his component fits into it. He should be able to develop his component with as little ongoing interchange with the rest of the team as possible. He has clear, precisely defined and diagrammed interfaces with the work of the others. When one programmer changes his design it should not affect the designs of the other programmers, unless this is unavoidable. The interfaces between the work of different programmers need to be unchanging. To achieve this requires high-precision techniques for designing the overall structure of the system.

THE HARDWARE
IMPLICATIONS

The manipulation of graphic images requires a personal computer with bit-mapped graphics, a mouse, and decisecond response times. The encyclopedia, however, requires large storage capacity and a larger computer because it is employing processing-intensive artificial-intelligence techniques and it is shared by many users. The machine environment for information engineering is a mainframe or central machine on which the encyclopedia is maintained, connected to workstations for planners, analysts, designers, management, and end users (Fig. 4.9).

The graphics workstation that the designer uses needs to have a mini-encyclopedia for the building of that designer's perspective. Subsets of the

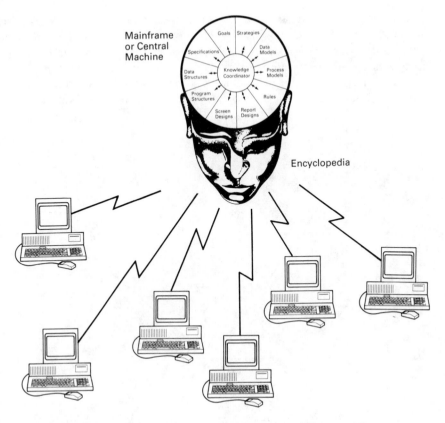

Workstations for Planners, Analysts, Designers, Programmers, and Management.

Figure 4.9   The environment of modern system design is a graphics workstation (usually, a personal computer) connected to a shared knowledgebase (usually, on a mainframe). Mini-encyclopedias with knowledge extracted from the
central encyclopedia reside in the local workstations.

mainframe knowledgebase are downloaded into the local workstation and its
mini-encyclopedia. When the designer has built a perspective it is uploaded to
the central repository for reconciliation of the new information with the old.

**THE
COORDINATION
OF PERSPECTIVES**
Information engineering is achieved by synthesizing
the knowledge and design of many people who may
be scattered across a large enterprise. A central encyclopedia is a repository of this knowledge. Com-
puterized tools are needed for helping to synthesize and coordinate the knowledge. The amount and complexity of information is so great that the synthesis
is a practical possibility only if computerized tools are used to achieve it.

Any one person or design team is not familiar with the entire set of designs in the central encyclopedia, but has one *perspective* of it. When the person starts to create a design he will extract whatever information in the central encyclopedia relates to his design. For example, he may extract a portion of a data model. He may be designing the detail of a process which is already shown in a higher-level representation. He then works on his design, largely indepen-

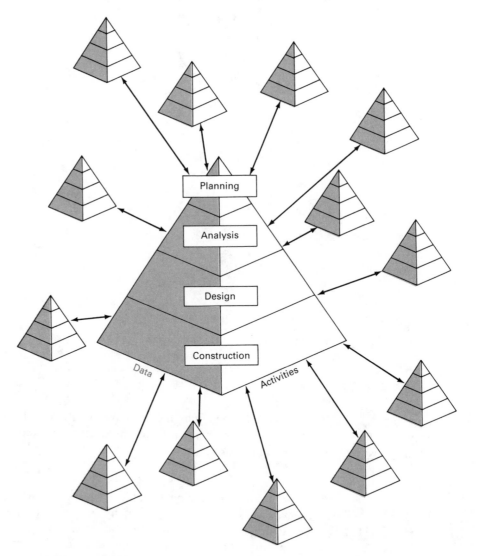

Figure 4.10 Design work takes place in localized mini-encyclopedias. The *perspectives* built in these local environments are coordinated with the knowledge in the central encyclopedia.

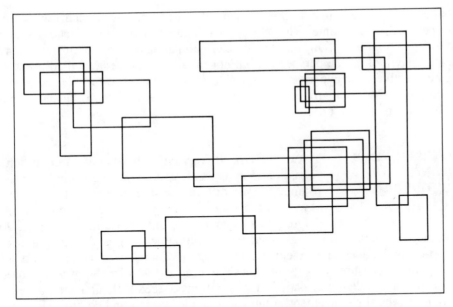

Figure 4.11   The perspectives of different designers have much overlap.

dently of the central encyclopedia. When the design is ready for review it can be coordinated, with computerized help, with the knowledge already in the encyclopedia.

The designer thus extracts information from the central encyclopedia into his mini-encyclopedia, works on it in a local environment, and then coordinates it with the knowledge in the central encyclopedia. When the design is coordinated and approved it will reside in the central encyclopedia and may affect the work of other designers. There may be many mini-encyclopedias, all being used in conjunction with the central encyclopedia, as illustrated in Fig. 4.10.

CONSISTENCY AMONG DIFFERENT ANALYSTS

Large projects are worked on by a team of analysts and implementers. Designs done by different people need to work together with absolute precision. It is very difficult to achieve this with manual methods. A good I-CASE tool enforces consistency among the work of different analysts and implementers. One of the major benefits of using I-CASE tools is this computerized enforcement of consistency among the different parts of the design as they evolve. The larger and more complex a project, the more it needs precise computerized coordination of the work of different implementers.

The central encyclopedia contains many *perspectives.* The various perspectives overlap; in other words, they use common objects and employ data derived from a common data model. One implementer (or sometimes a team) works on one perspective at a time. This perspective contains multiple objects, associations, diagrams, notes, and text which can be manipulated by its *owner*. Many people may look at the perspective but not modify it. These are called *users* of the perspective. The hyperview perspective may record the *knowledge source*— an end user, end-user group, joint application design workshop, business area analysis team, and so on.

CONSISTENCY AMONG MULTIPLE PROJECTS

A computerized corporation has many different databases and systems. It is necessary to achieve consistency among different systems because they interact with one another in complex ways. Systems in different plants and locations transmit information to one another. Data is often extracted from multiple systems and aggregated for purposes of business management. Different locations need commonality of management measurements. Sometimes the term *corporate transparency* is used to mean that detailed information in all locations is accessible in a computerized form to a central management group for decision-support and control purposes.

CASE tools make it practical to achieve consistency among multiple projects. Designs for different systems are derived from common data models and process models, which are available to implementers from the encyclopedia.

THE KNOWLEDGE COORDINATOR

An integral part of encyclopedia-based systems is a *knowledge coordinator*. The knowledge coordinator is software which ensures consistency among the different pieces of knowledge that reside in the encyclopedia. It applies artificial-intelligence rules to the information that is checked into the encyclopedia. When a person using a workstation enters new information into that workstation, the knowledge coordinator checks that it obeys the rules and is consistent with what is already in the encyclopedia.

A person using an I-CASE workstation builds his own model or design. This is represented in a local hyperdiagram. The knowledge coordinator enforces consistency within that hyperdiagram. The local hyperdiagram is built with objects which are extracted from a central encyclopedia and use the detail that is centrally stored. There is, thus, consistency between the local representation and the central representation.

The person at the workstation may create new objects, new associations, or new detail. This will eventually be entered into the central encyclopedia. The knowledge coordinator then has the task of ensuring that the local perspective is consistent with the central information. It will indicate any inconsistencies, and these must be corrected. The local workstation user will normally correct the inconsistencies arising from his work. Sometimes a central administrator has to resolve conflicts about how objects are designed or described.

Two implementers may create two separate perspectives. The knowledge coordinator has the task of examining them in combination to ensure complete consistency between them. In this way, consistency is achieved even in a multiperson project or in a multiproject environment. Incompatibility is minimized by employing the descriptions of data and other objects which are already in the central encyclopedia, whenever possible.

There are usually multiple versions of a design. The workbench should enable multiple versions of perspectives to be stored and archived. The graphics representations on the screen should be able to show all inconsistencies between two perspectives or between versions of the same perspective. This may be done with highlighting, reverse video, or color.

The techniques for coordinating the perspectives and building consistency are discussed in Book III. An important aspect of these techniques is to *solve local problems locally wherever possible*. It is difficult or impossible to achieve consistency among the work of many analysts or implementers with manual techniques. A computer with CASE representations can enforce absolute consistency. Achieving consistency becomes a human problem of resolving different opinions rather than a technical problem of detecting inconsistencies. The computerized corporation of the future will not be built without computerized enforcement of consistency among its many information systems.

LAYERS OF INTEGRITY CHECKING AND ANALYSIS

The axioms and rules that a computer can apply to the work of the designers and planners are built up in layers as shown in Fig. 4.12. First they can be applied to a single diagram to make it complete and consistent. Then they can be applied to the combination of information from multiple diagram types which form the hyperdiagram. The hyperdiagram is made complete and consistent in its own right. Next, the information in the hyperdiagram is coordinated with that of other perspectives. At each of these stages rule processing using artificial intelligence techniques can be applied. A dialog with the designer will take place in which the computer asks for information it needs to complete its knowledge of a perspective or to deal with inconsistencies.

A variety of analysis tools are required for the synthesis of different data views, different perspectives, and different types of planning information. The outer layer of Fig. 4.12 relates to the types of analysis, discussed in Books II and III, which are applied to the knowledge in the encyclopedia.

The central encyclopedia may be associated with layers of software as shown in Fig. 4.13. The outermost layer of that figure represents the tools that the designer uses to create diagrams. As well as providing the tools for drawing

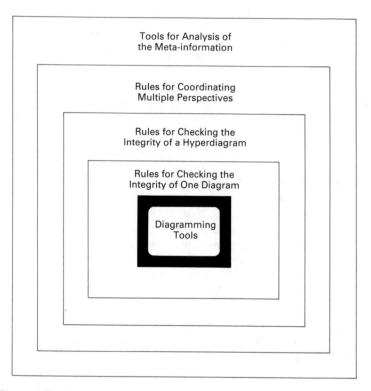

Figure 4.12   Axioms and rules are used for checking first a single diagram, then the group of diagrams that combine to create a hyperdiagram, then the coordination of multiple perspectives across the enterprise. A variety of analysis tools are needed to help build the combinations of perspectives for the overall pyramid, and to aid planners in growing the information resources of the enterprise.

and collecting relevant detail, this software needs to employ rule-based processing to link the diagrams logically to form a perspective and provide a thorough set of integrity checks on the perspective.

The next layer is a knowledge coordinator needed to check the consistency of multiple perspectives. New perspectives may be checked against the knowledge already in the encyclopedia. Perspectives created by different designers are coordinated. A designer may be shown graphically how his design conflicts with other perspectives.

The third layer represents tools for central analysis of the overall collection of knowledge. These tools may operate in a batch fashion. They may be used for planning purposes or to assist in the overall migration toward better coordinated systems. This layer may provide library functions or assist in the checking out and checking in of perspectives from the central encyclopedia.

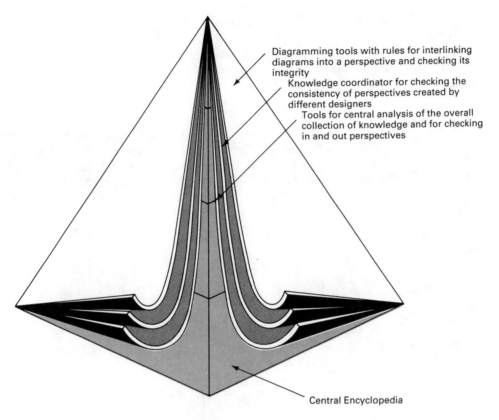

Diagramming tools with rules for interlinking diagrams into a perspective and checking its integrity

Knowledge coordinator for checking the consistency of perspectives created by different designers

Tools for central analysis of the overall collection of knowledge and for checking in and out perspectives

Central Encyclopedia

Figure 4.13

STEAL;
DON'T REINVENT

A basic principle of any form of engineering ought to be: "Steal; don't reinvent." If something already exists and works well, it is desirable to use it rather than to reinvent an alternative and have to wrestle with new design and implementation. A workbench tool should enable designers to capture already existing segments of design, programs, and knowledge. This can save much work and greatly lessens the problems with incompatibility. Reusable design should be the way of life in information engineering wherever practical.

Without information engineering tools, most application designers work on their own and so often reinvent the wheel. Copying objects or designs already in the encyclopedia helps to eliminate the mass of avoidable conflicts, redundancies, and misunderstandings that happen when people work in mutual isolation. When a designer first loads his own mini-encyclopedia from the central encyclopedia he may ask for selected objects and relationships, for a whole diagram, for all the objects and relationships in a given perspective, or for all the objects on which the encyclopedia is in disagreement with his perspective.

Tools such as these are likely to increase the employment of reusable code and reusable designs. This subject is discussed in detail in Book III. It has a great effect on overall I.S. productivity.

BRIDGES BETWEEN INCOMPATIBLE PERSPECTIVES

Sometimes a perspective cannot be changed, at least not quickly. Sometimes a design is frozen while the programming of that system is done. The objects are software modules or packages that cannot be modified. The encyclopedia should have knowledge about what can and cannot be modified.

Often a bridge is needed between subsystems which are incompatible.

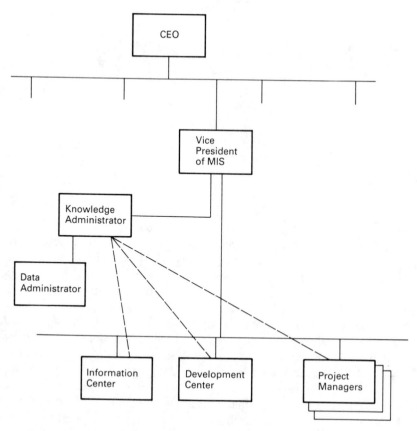

Figure 4.14 The keeper of the encyclopedia may be called the knowledge administrator. He needs to report at a suitably high level.

Good design has uncomplicated interfaces. The bridge ought to be no more than the conversion of data that pass from one subsystem to another. The encyclopedia should make clear the different incompatible versions of data, and the diagrams should show the data conversions necessary to build bridges between separate perspectives.

THE KNOWLEDGE   As discussed in Chapter 3, there is now much expe-
ADMINISTRATOR   rience of data administration in many corporations
[5]. The data administrator has the task of coordinating the logical representations of the corporation's data. An extension of this task is the coordination of perspectives (like those of Fig. 4.11), and for the general coordination of what is in the encyclopedia. We will refer to the person responsible for this task as the *knowledge administrator;* sometimes the term *encyclopedia administrator* has been used, sometimes *development coordinator*.

Data administration, an important task, is a subset of the task of administering the overall contents of the encyclopedia. The knowledge administrator may have a data administrator working for him, or the data administrator may have been promoted to the larger task of being the knowledge administrator.

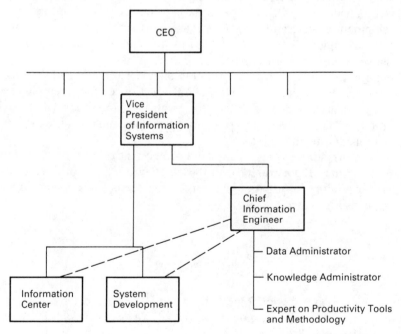

Figure 4.15   The chief information engineer may employ a data administrator and knowledge administrator who coordinate the data models and perspectives in the encyclopedia.

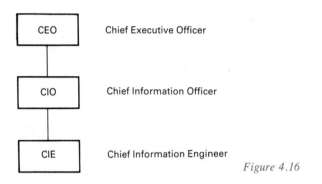

Figure 4.16

Like the data administrator, the knowledge administrator needs computerized tools to help him analyze and coordinate the knowledge. He will examine many perspectives, helping to synthesize them into as consistent a whole as possible.

Like the data administrator, the knowledge administrator ought to report at a suitably high level. Figure 4.14 shows the knowledge administrator reporting to the vice-president of MIS. He has a dashed-line link to the information center, development center, and to project managers, and is responsible for ensuring that they employ the encyclopedia, link into the data model and that the best possible coordination of perspectives is achieved.

Figure 4.15 shows a chief information engineer reporting to the vice-president of information systems. The chief information engineer employs a data administrator, a knowledge administrator, who tries to achieve the maximum coordination of perspectives, and possibly specialists such as an expert on productivity tools and methodology.

Chief information engineer may be an important title in the corporation of the future. He may report directly to the chief information officer, who is responsible for relating information systems to the needs and opportunities of the business, as in Fig. 4.16.

REFERENCES

1. James Martin and Carma McClure, *Action Diagrams: Clearly Structured Specifications, Programs, and Procedures, Second Edition,* Prentice-Hall, Inc., Englewood Cliffs, NJ, 1989.

2. James Martin, *Recommended Diagramming Standards for Analysts and Programmers,* Prentice-Hall, Inc., Englewood Cliffs, NJ, 1987.

3. James Martin and Carma McClure, *Diagramming Techniques for Analysts and Programmers,* Prentice-Hall, Inc., Englewood Cliffs, NJ, 1985.

4. IEW (Information Engineering Workbench) from KnowledgeWare, Atlanta, GA, uses several thousand rules programmed with AI techniques for checking the perspectives built in a PC.

5. James Martin, *Managing the Data-Base Environment,* Prentice-Hall, Inc., Englewood Cliffs, NJ, 1983.

5 THE STAGES OF INFORMATION ENGINEERING

INTRODUCTION   As noted earlier information engineering has four discrete phases—the four levels of the pyramid.

- Strategy
- Analysis
- Design
- Construction

The construction phase should cover the fielding and deployment of systems. The maintenance of systems, and the migration from non-IE systems to the new IE environment, are extremely important, but ought to be dealt with *using the same basic four layers* of the pyramid.

One of the objectives of information engineering is the automation of the I.S. process, using computers to lessen the paperwork burden. As we achieve a higher level of automation some of the procedures of the earlier manual age can be eliminated. It is desirable to avoid bureaucracy and time-consuming paperwork.

The four levels are represented by four stages, summarized earlier, as follows:

Stage 1: Information Strategy Planning. Concerned with top management goals and critical success factors. Concerned with how technology can be used to create new opportunities or competitive advantages. A high-level overview is created of the enterprise, its functions, data, and information needs.

Stage 2: Business Area Analysis. Concerned with *what* processes are needed to run a selected business area, how these processes interrelate, and what data are needed. A fully normalized data model is built. The process model is mapped against the data model.

Stage 3: System Design. Concerned with *how* selected processes in the business area are implemented in procedures, and how the procedures work. Direct end-user involvement is needed in the design of procedures and interaction with prototypes.

Stage 4: Construction. Implementation of the procedures using, where practical, code generators and end-user tools. Design is linked to construction by means of prototyping.

Diagrams are important in each of the stages. Figure 4.8 summarized the types of diagrams that may be employed at each stage.

STAGE 1: INFORMATION STRATEGY PLANNING

An enterprise normally begins the information engineering process by developing an information strategy plan. The information strategy plan is concerned with the goals and targets of the business and with how technology can be used to create new opportunities or competitive advantages. Technological opportunities are identified. Critical success factors for the enterprise are decomposed into critical success factors for the divisions and then related to the motivations of executives.

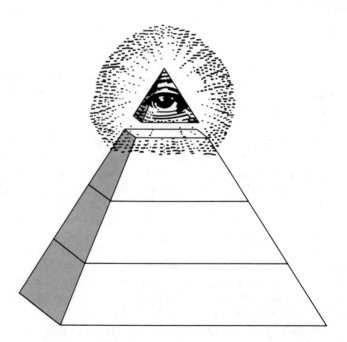

The information strategy plan maps the basic functions of the enterprise and produces a high-level model of the enterprise, its departments, its functions, and its data. It creates an overview entity-relationship diagram and maps the entity types to the functions of the enterprise.

At the top of the information engineering pyramid two types of studies are carried out (Fig. 5.1):

- A determination of the strategic opportunities, goals, critical success factors, and information needs of different parts of the enterprise. A determination of how new technologies might be used to meet the goals better and create new business opportunities

- The creation of an overview model of the enterprise, and the splitting of this into areas appropriate for business area analysis

The first of these is an analysis of how the enterprise functions; the second is a management-oriented study of how it might be made to function better with the help of technology. These studies can be thought of independently, although they are often done by the same team at the same time. Doing them concurrently enables information for both to be gathered in the same management interviews, thereby minimizing the management time involved. The studies are strongly related. As the overview of the enterprise and its goals emerge, ways of restructuring the enterprise may become apparent which enable it to meet its goals better.

Box 5.1 lists the objectives of information strategy planning. This set of

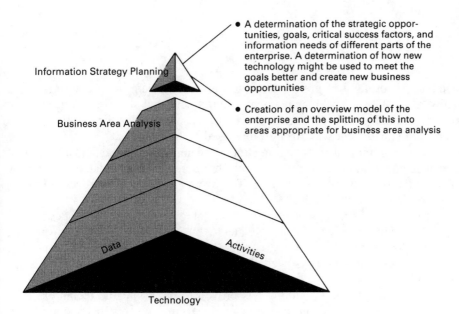

Figure 5.1   At the top of the pyramid two types of studies are carried out.

BOX 5.1 Objectives of information strategy planning

- Investigate how better use of technology can enable an enterprise to gain competitive advantage.
- Establish goals for the enterprise and critical success factors.
- Use critical success factor analysis for steering the enterprise to enable it to better achieve its goals.
- Determine what information can enable management to perform its work better.
- Prioritize the building of information systems in terms of their overall effect on the bottom line.
- Create an overview model of the enterprise, its processes, and information.
- Subdivide the overview model into business areas ready for business area analysis (level 2 of the pyramid).
- Determine which business areas to analyze first.
- Enable top management to view its enterprise in terms of goals, functions, information, critical success factors, and organization structure.

This set of objectives is normally of great interest to top management.

objectives is normally of great interest to top management in an enterprise, and usually to the CEO. Top management commitment and support are needed for information engineering. The most successful case examples tend to be those in which top management was strongly involved.

It is important that information strategy planning be understandable to both top management and end users. It should be reviewed and updated continually as part of the business planning cycle. The results should be recorded and maintained continually in the encyclopedia.

Box 5.2 lists the steps of information strategy planning. The upper part of Box 5.2 contains the steps which relate to business strategy; the lower part relates to the technical IE infrastructure. Different enterprises use somewhat different steps, so flexibility is needed in the software tools used for information strategy planning.

Information strategy planning has proven to be a valuable technique even when the other phases of information engineering have not been completed. With information strategy planning, top management's attention is focused on

BOX 5.2   Steps in information strategy planning

(The steps used vary from one enterprise to another and hence need flexibility in the planning software tools.)

Business Oriented

- Computerize the organization chart of the enterprise.
- Identify the organization's goals, targets, and strategies.
- Examine technological trends and how they might be used by the enterprise to create new opportunities or competitive advantages.
- Determine critical success factors for the enterprise and break these down into critical success factors throughout the organization chart.
- Interview key executives to determine problems, opportunities, and information needs.
- Record all of the above in a computerized planning and analysis tool.

Technology Oriented

- Develop an enterprise model showing the basic functions of the enterprise on a function decomposition diagram.
- Develop an overview entity model.
- Analyze the functions and entities with a matrix tool and determine business areas (ready for level 2 of the pyramid: business area analysis).
- Analyze current systems.
- Set priorities for information system development.

technological opportunities and on what is happening within the enterprise. In fact, it has often resulted in organizational restructuring.

Most businesses have a business plan which is updated periodically and is concerned with setting targets, goals, and strategies. The planning process may analyze the trends in the industry, technology, and competition. Top management planning sessions should use the information in the encyclopedia and encourage regular review of the goals and critical success factors. The hierarchy of critical success factors should be related to the motivation of employees via management by objectives, thereby establishing a mechanism for steering the entire organization toward the achievement of its goals.

Business strategy planning, then, forms a basic input to the top level of

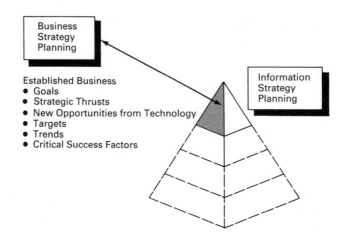

Figure 5.2   Information for business strategy planning resides in the encyclopedia for the uppermost layer of the pyramid.

the pyramid (Fig. 5.2). Figure 5.3 shows some of the computerized charts used in information strategy planning (ISP).

The time taken to do an ISP has typically ranged from 3 to 12 months. In one large oil company of great complexity it took 9 months and involved nine high executives on a part-time basis. If an ISP takes longer than 12 months to do, something is wrong. Six months is a reasonable target in a medium-sized enterprise. It happens faster when the person responsible for it knows exactly what to do or has professional consulting help. He needs computerized tools and needs to solicit the help of key top executives. This is likely to happen only if the top executive is committed to the project and understands its potential benefits.

An ISP is not frozen when it is finished. It produces a collection of knowledge which is valuable in running the enterprise, setting its goals, and determining how to meet those goals. Information from this part of the encyclopedia is valuable at top-level planning sessions. Some corporations review critical success factors at board meetings. The section of the encyclopedia storing the ISP should be made accessible and updatable on an ongoing basis. Like the rest of the encyclopedia, it is a valuable corporate asset.

STAGE 2: BUSINESS AREA ANALYSIS

Top top-level planning determines which business areas should be the first targets for business area analysis. The overall objective of this second stage of information engineering is to understand what processes and data are necessary to make the enterprise work and to determine how these processes and data interrelate.

In this stage of information engineering, a fully normalized data model is developed; the functions identified in the first stage are decomposed into processes; a process dependency diagram is drawn showing how the processes interrelate; and a matrix is built to show what data entities are used, updated, and created through what processes. Figure 5.4 shows the types of diagrams used.

Again, the information represented in diagrams on the workstation screen is stored and updated in the encyclopedia. The encyclopedia is designed to aid in the collection of data and in the application of integrity controls. When stage 2 is complete, a structured graphic description, designed with an interlocking mesh of cross-checks, exists for the enterprise and its organization, goals, data, and processes.

A typical business area analysis takes three to six months. The procedure is made practical by dividing the business into areas sufficiently small that they can be analyzed in this time. Earlier attempts to do normalized data models of entire enterprises sometimes failed because of the magnitude of the task. It is better to do one area at a time, picking the more important areas first.

Business area analysis should be independent of the technology the enterprise might use. Technology is changing fast. This level of the pyramid is concerned with the fundamental data needed and the fundamental processes that the enterprise must carry out. The data will still be needed and the processes must still be performed even if great technological change occurs. Level 2 of the pyramid is concerned with *what* is needed, and level 3 is concerned with *how* systems are implemented.

Business area analysis should also be independent of current systems. The old systems in use in an enterprise often constrain it to use inefficient procedures with batch processing, dumb terminals, unnecessary keypunching, redundancy, too much paperwork, and the bureaucracy that goes with paperwork. Entirely different procedures may be designed if there can be a personal computer on every knowledge worker's desk, on-line to databases anywhere in the enterprise. Fundamental analysis of *what* processes are needed often causes a fundamental rethinking of what is the best way to implement them.

Business area analysis has the following characteristics:

- It is conducted separately for each business area.
- It creates a detailed data model for the business area.
- It creates a detailed process model and links it to the data model.
- The results are recorded and maintained in the encyclopedia.
- It requires intensive user involvement.
- It remains independent of technology.
- It remains independent of current systems and procedures.
- It often causes a rethinking of systems and procedures.
- It identifies areas for system design.

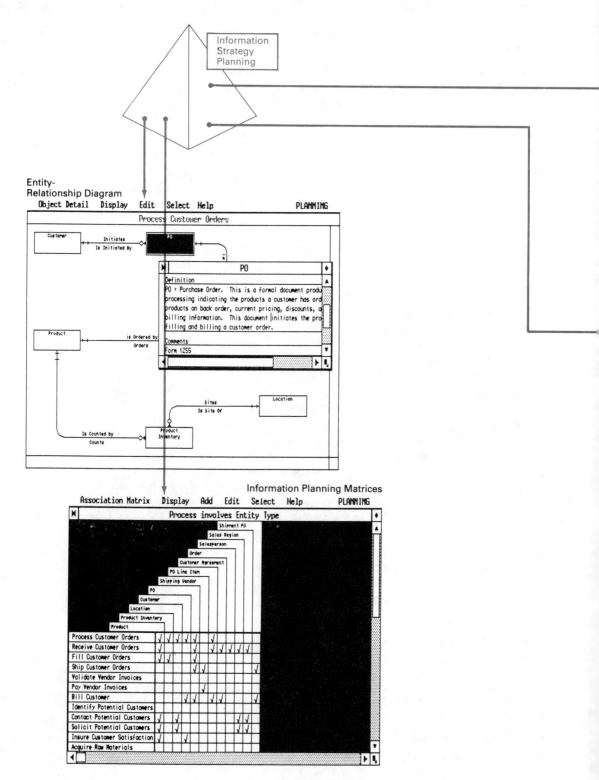

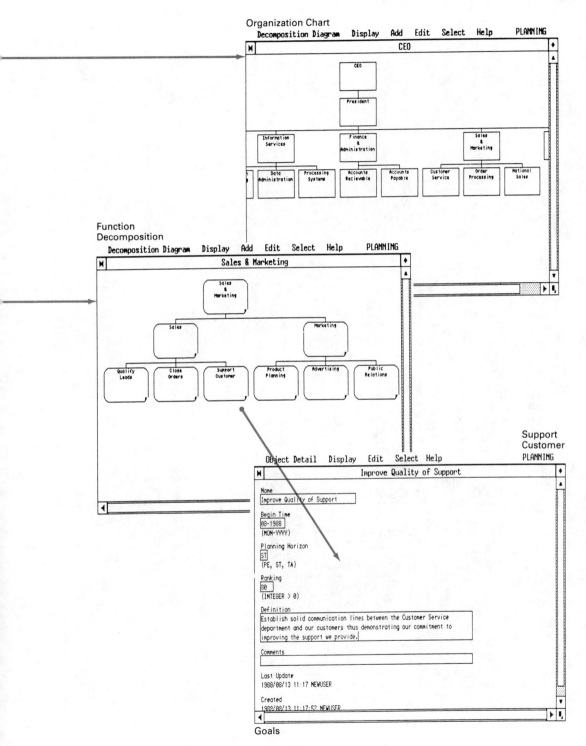

Organization Chart

Function Decomposition

Support Customer

Goals

Figure 5.3   (Continued)

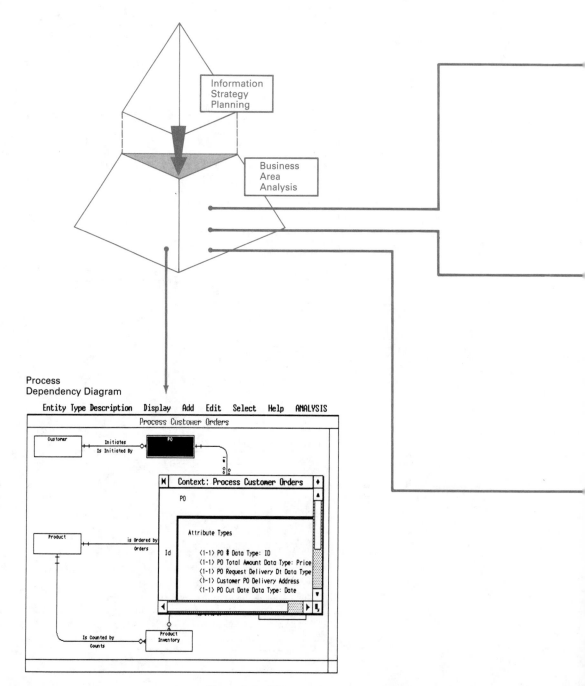

Figure 5.4 Diagrams used in business area analysis.

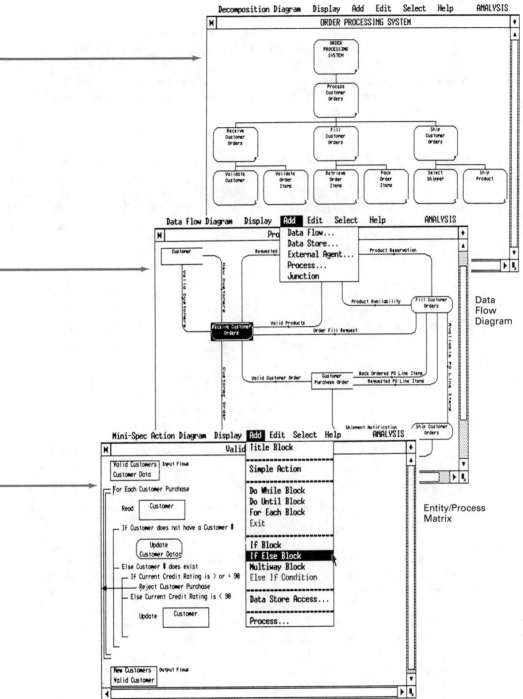

Process
Decomposition Diagram

Data
Flow
Diagram

Entity/Process
Matrix

Figure 5.4 (Continued)

The information collected in the encyclopedia in the two top stages of information engineering gives an overview that can be analyzed and cross-checked in many ways. A variety of rules are applied by the knowledge coordinator of the encyclopedia. The information can be collected at different times and can be assembled in different ways. Steadily, the computerized knowledge of the enterprise becomes more complete.

STAGE 3: SYSTEM DESIGN   When a business area analysis has been completed, system design can proceed relatively quickly, and separately designed systems can be linked to benefit the enterprise. Particularly important, the end users should be as deeply involved as possible in the design process. This level of involvement can be achieved in a variety of ways, all of which are described in detail in Book III.

- Teach users to design their own procedures with easy-to-use graphics tools.
- Use prototyping.
- Establish information center activities.
- Conduct joint application design sessions.

Objectives of the system design stage are as follows:

- Involve the end users fully in the design process.
- Speed up design and implementation.
- Make systems flexible and easy to change.
- Automate the design, documentation, and maintenance.
- Base the design on the encyclopedia.
- Link design automation to fourth-generation languages or code generation.
- Create and evolve prototypes.

System design changed dramatically when design-automation tools became available. With these tools, design work is accelerated because the design is created on a computer screen rather than at a drawing board with pencils and plastic templates. The designer can constantly edit the design, adding and changing blocks and links, cutting and pasting, and enhancing detail. The computer provides details of data and interfaces from the encyclopedia, guides the designer, and verifies the design through integrity checks. The designer must create a well-structured design; the tools enforce this.

The main types of diagrams used in structured system design are decomposition diagrams, action diagrams, dependency or data-flow diagrams, data–structure diagrams, screen layouts, and report layouts. In some circumstances it is useful to employ decision trees or state-transition diagrams. All of these diagrams can be created with a common family of symbols. The diagrams are associated with pop-up screen windows asking the designer to fill in details or displaying details not shown on the diagram. The objective of using diagrams with associated detail windows is to collect enough data in the encyclopedia to form a basis for code generation.

Figure 5.5 illustrates diagrams used in systems design. The encyclopedia applies many rules to these diagrams to enforce integrity. The diagrams are tightly interlinked so that they form a unified body of knowledge—the perspective described in Chapter 4. The diagrams of business area analysis (Fig. 5.4) form a high-level perspective. This is used in creating the more detailed perspectives of system design.

STAGE 4: CONSTRUCTION

The design, created at a design workbench, should be taken directly into a code generator. As we have emphasized, the code generator should be coupled directly to the design workbench, with its diagrams of programs, screen designs, report designs, database accesses, and subroutine calls. The specifications and diagrams built at the design workbench screen should be detailed enough to eliminate the need for coding with mnemonics. The constructs used by the code generator should be represented in mouse menus so that they can be quickly added into the action diagrams that represent the design.

A key object of I-CASE tools is to impose rules on data modeling and procedure design that are formal enough to direct the *computer* to write code, thus freeing I.S. professionals from the time-consuming tasks of writing and debugging code. It is important to note that the four-stage information engineering process described here requires that much more time be spent on planning and design than on execution. In traditional systems development, time and effort are heavily skewed to coding. This creates a "chicken-and-egg" problem, miring MIS professionals more deeply into the development backlog—an endless cycle of poor planning feeding inadequate design, resulting in systems that do not meet business needs and require major revisions and maintenance (i.e., *more coding*). The lack of automated tools for systems development has aggravated this problem.

Information engineering attacks the backlog problem in several ways:

- Development is fast because of automated tools.
- Users are directly involved in the design process so that it meets their needs directly (see Book III).
- Quality systems are built, requiring less revision and maintenance.
- Most modifications to procedures can be made quickly and easily.
- End users are encouraged to generate their reports and use computers directly with end-user languages and tools.

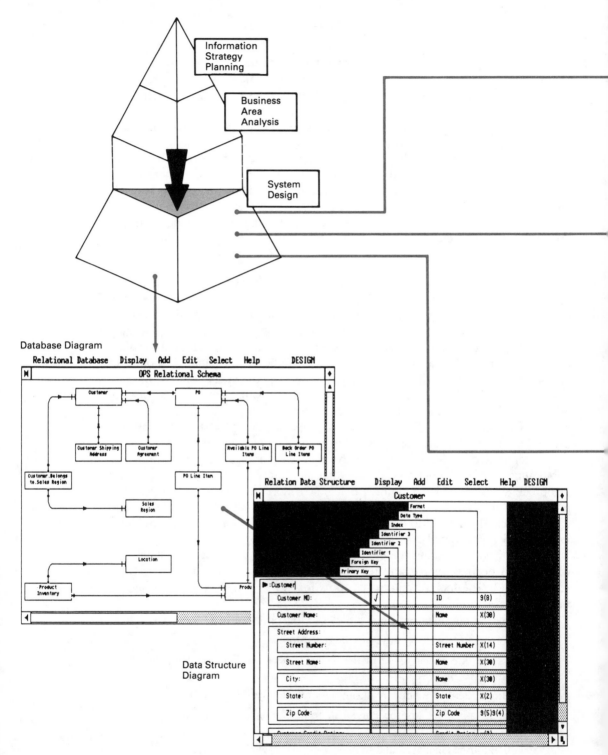

Figure 5.5 Some of the diagrams used in system design.

Structure Chart Diagram

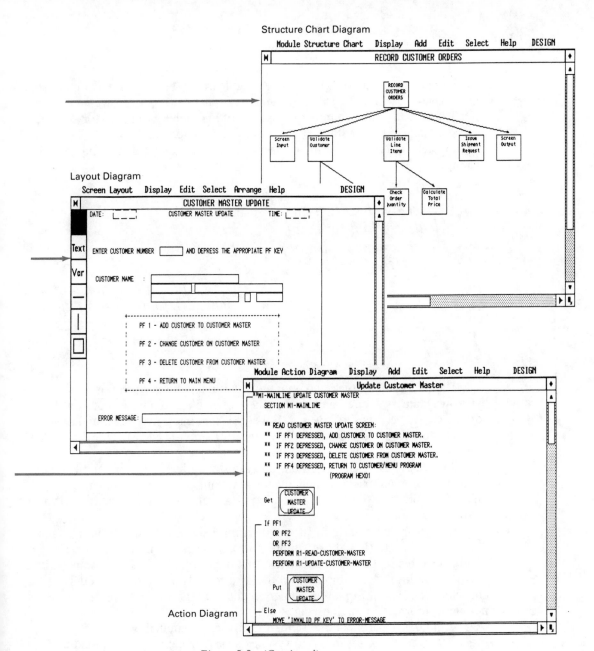

Layout Diagram

Action Diagram

Figure 5.5   (Continued)

Increasing numbers of end users are learning how to use computerized tools. These users can access databases, generate reports, and manipulate spreadsheets. A smaller number of users build complex programs for statistical analysis, financial modeling, engineering computation, and so on. The spread of computer skills and information centers is a valuable aid to better decision making.

> *Give a man a fish and*
> *you feed him for a day.*
> *Teach a man to fish and*
> *you feed him for life.*

> *Give a user a program and*
> *you satisfy him for a day.*
> *Teach a user to program and*
> *you satisfy him for life.*

The danger of end-user computing is that many tools permit users to create their own data structures and design their own files. If this is not controlled, corporate data becomes a Tower of Babel. System integrity is lost, and management cannot extract and process the vital information needed for top-level planning.

Some end users add to their programs a little at a time, until a large spaghetti-like mass exists, undocumented and unmaintainable. Sometimes, multiple copies are used in different locations without much comprehension of how the program works.

It is clear that management and discipline are needed in end-user computing. The discipline should not suppress inventiveness or initiative because it is highly desirable that users be creative about their organization's procedures. The answer is to link user computing to the data models and process models in the encyclopedia. The information center should manage the linkage of user computing to information engineering.

Although departmental systems or personal computation may be done by users, more complex systems and systems spanning departments should be built by data processing professionals, with strong end-user participation through workshops and prototyping. Action diagrams are designed to be easily understood by users and to represent the structures of structured design. The same form of diagram is used for both specifications and coding. With a computerized editor, the specification is decomposed into a program, with the action diagram editor set to create the control constructs of a chosen language (Fig. 5.6).

Other diagrams used for system design should be automatically convertible into action diagrams. The knowledge in the encyclopedia is built up by means

SPECIFICATION

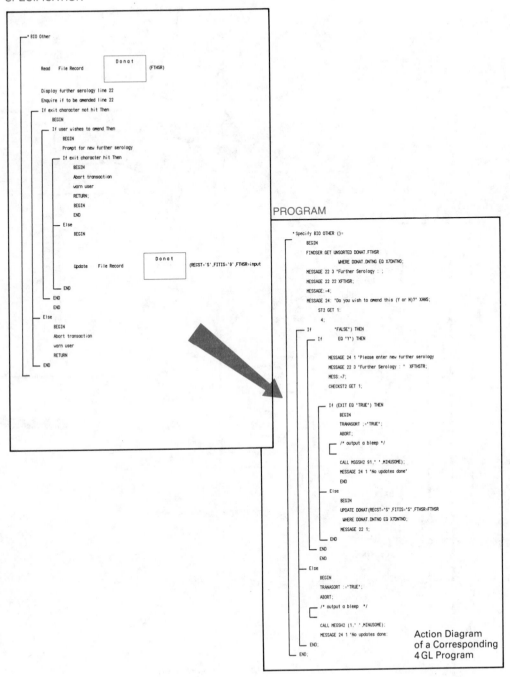

PROGRAM

Figure 5.6 An action diagram of a specification can be successively expanded into more detail and become a corresponding program.

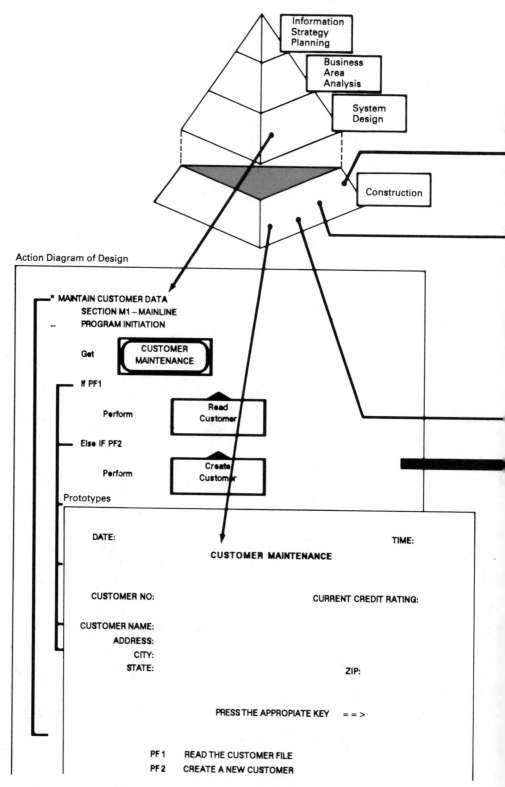

Figure 5.7 Diagrams used at the construction stage.

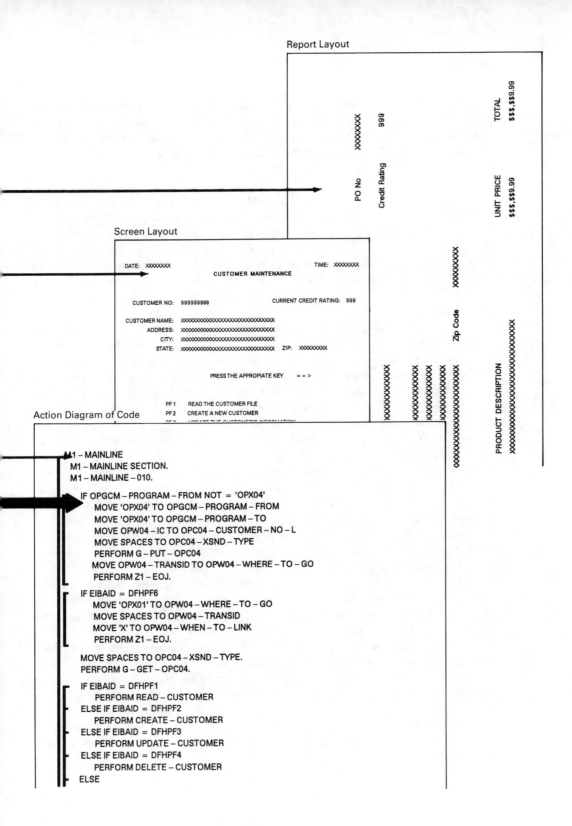

Report Layout

Screen Layout

Action Diagram of Code

```
M1 – MAINLINE
M1 – MAINLINE SECTION.
M1 – MAINLINE – 010.

    IF OPGCM – PROGRAM – FROM NOT = 'OPX04'
        MOVE 'OPX04' TO OPGCM – PROGRAM – FROM
        MOVE 'OPX04' TO OPGCM – PROGRAM – TO
        MOVE OPW04 – IC TO OPC04 – CUSTOMER – NO – L
        MOVE SPACES TO OPC04 – XSND – TYPE
        PERFORM G – PUT – OPC04
        MOVE OPW04 – TRANSID TO OPW04 – WHERE – TO – GO
        PERFORM Z1 – EOJ.

    IF EIBAID = DFHPF6
        MOVE 'OPX01' TO OPW04 – WHERE – TO – GO
        MOVE SPACES TO OPW04 – TRANSID
        MOVE 'X' TO OPW04 – WHEN – TO – LINK
        PERFORM Z1 – EOJ.

    MOVE SPACES TO OPC04 – XSND – TYPE.
    PERFORM G – GET – OPC04.

    IF EIBAID = DFHPF1
        PERFORM READ – CUSTOMER
    ELSE IF EIBAID = DFHPF2
        PERFORM CREATE – CUSTOMER
    ELSE IF EIBAID = DFHPF3
        PERFORM UPDATE – CUSTOMER
    ELSE IF EIBAID = DFHPF4
        PERFORM DELETE – CUSTOMER
    ELSE
```

Figure 5.7   (Continued)

of design diagrams, and the encyclopedia generates a corresponding action diagram. This diagram can then be edited on the screen and converted into code, along with the corresponding data structure, screen layout, and report layout. Figure 5.7 shows the diagrams used at the construction stage.

**END-USER
INVOLVEMENT
AT EVERY LEVEL**
Traditional techniques for application development often resulted in systems mismatched to the needs of end users. In the worst cases, multimillion-dollar systems were rejected or bypassed by end users. Along with automated development techniques, we must have techniques for better meeting the true needs of end users. The most powerful of these techniques are prototyping and workshops in which end users and I.S. professionals jointly create plans and designs.

A basic principle of information engineering is that end users should be involved at every stage. Technical professionals often convince themselves that they know what end users need. In practice it is extremely difficult for a technical professional to understand what is in the head of a financial professional and vice versa. The subtleties of how a factory shop floor operates are known only by the people who work on the shop floor. Different professionals have complex knowledge of their own area and only superficial knowledge of other disciplines. To build good systems, we have to harness the knowledge of diverse professionals who have different cultures. This is best done in a workshop environment using diagrams that all the professionals can understand.

At the highest level the goal is to understand the enterprise and how technology might improve it. This requires highly creative interaction between top management and top technical personnel.

At the analysis level the goal is to build models of the processes and data needed to run the enterprise, in such a way that these models provide a framework for developing cleanly engineered systems that can evolve rapidly to meet changing needs. The data models incorporate many business rules describing how the business functions. Experience with much modeling has shown that a key to success is strong end-user involvement so that end users check the models to ensure that they reflect the real world correctly.

At the design level, users should be involved in a requirements planning workshop and a design workshop. The design workshop creates a design, using an IE workbench, which can be quickly constructed with a code generator. An objective is not only to meet the needs of the users better, but also to speed up the traditional design process.

At the construction level selected users may review prototypes that evolve in functionality until the final system can be created from them. When major maintenance is done, a user workshop may identify what modifications to the system are needed, and design the modification. Users should be involved in prototyping the modifications.

I-CASE tools facilitate prototyping. At a low level of prototyping report designers and screen painters are used so that end users can look at the reports or sequence of screens that they will receive. At a somewhat higher level, portions of applications can be created quickly, but without the ability to handle errors, exception conditions, recovery, security, high performance, and so on. The users work with the screens, reports, and applications and often suggest modifications and additions. Many changes may be made as prototypes evolve from an initial design concept to mature designs. Multiple design iterations, carried out quickly with strong user involvement, help ensure that truly valuable systems are implemented.

JOINT APPLICATION DESIGN

A particularly valuable technique is joint application design (JAD) [1]. With JAD, a design workshop is held in which end users are the main participants in design development. Data processing professionals are present to assist the users, and a session leader ensures that the procedure is carried out in a thorough and orderly manner. The users are guided through the system design procedure and are encouraged to express their needs and concerns as a design emerges.

JAD works much better when automated tools are used. As the workshop participants sketch aspects of the design on a white board and adjust them, a CASE tool operator (often referred to as the "scribe") enters the information into the CASE tool. A computable design is built up. Parts of the design can be printed out for the participants to study and mark up when appropriate. Sometimes a large-screen projector is used to show the CASE diagrams to the group. JAD using computerized tools is sometimes referred to as *interactive JAD*. See Boxes 5.3 and 5.4.

An interactive JAD session creates report designs, screen layouts, and specifications in a CASE format that will link to a code generator. Where appropriate, prototypes are built during the JAD session.

In practice, JAD results not only in designs that meet the end users' needs better, it accelerates the design process. Instead of text specifications that end users have difficulty critiquing, it creates specifications that are structured, maintainable, and which lead to code generation. JAD should be part of information engineering, and this is referred to as IE/JAD. Unlike much of the *ad hoc* system building that occurs today, IE/JAD anchors the procedure into the management goals information already collected in information strategy planning, as well as into the computerized data models and process models developed in business area analysis.

In traditional system development, documentation takes much time and is usually poorly done. Statistics show that on large systems, more time is spent on documentation than on coding. With information engineering, most of the design documentation is gathered automatically in the encyclopedia and is re-

BOX 5.3 What is interactive JAD?

Interactive JAD

- Is a design workshop.
- Is comprised of end-user personnel with I.S. participation.
- Is conducted by a skilled session leader.
- Uses CASE tools.
- Should be part of information engineering.

It creates

- Screen designs
- Report designs
- Specifications in action diagram format
- Documentation in the encyclopedia
- Tested prototypes

BOX 5.4 Objectives and benefits of interactive JAD

- Ensure that end users are responsible for system specifications
- Improve design quality and usability
- Accelerate the design process
- Build easily maintainable applications
- Link design effort to management goals expressed in the encyclopedia
- Ensure integration with other IE systems by using the data models and process models in the encyclopedia
- Use design automation
- Create and adjust prototypes
- Document the design in the encyclopedia
- Create a design for which code can be generated where possible

corded in a more complete, structured fashion than is possible in traditional design.

The designer may store comments in the encyclopedia along with the other details the computer must process. The diagrams and comments developed at the computer screen are the documentation. Associated with these diagrams are the dictionary, data models, and process models. The computer asks the designer for the details it requires as the design proceeds.

WORKSHOPS AT ALL LEVELS

JAD-like workshops are valuable at the planning, analysis, and design levels of information engineering, as illustrated in Fig. 5.8. At the top management level formal techniques (discussed in Book II) have been used to identify critical success factors and the potential impact of technology, and then conduct management focusing workshops to make top management aware of the potential and determine what actions to take. In one large bank the specialist in conducting JAD workshops conducted one-day workshops for the CEO and top vice-presidents to determine what actions should be taken about using information technology to make the bank more profitable [2].

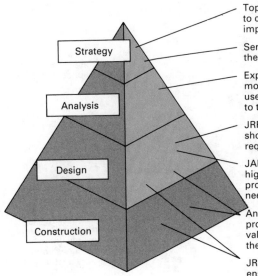

Top management workshops should be used to clarify how technology can be used to improve the enterprise.

Senior staff assistance is needed in modeling the enterprise.

Experience with data modeling and process modeling shows that a key to success is end-user participation in checking and helping add to the models.

JRP (Joint Requirements Planning) workshops should be of help with end users to determine the required functionality of a system.

JAD (Joint Application Design) workshops are a highly effective way of accelerating the design process and ensuring that it meets end-user needs as well as possible.

An end-user board should review evolving prototypes to ensure that the system is as valuable to them as possible and to help create the requisite training and changes in procedure.

JRP, JAD, and prototyping should be used to ensure that major maintenance changes meet end-user needs.

Figure 5.8 At each level in IE, strong user involvement is needed. This is often accomplished by the use of structured workshops in which appropriate sections of the IE encyclopedia are added to.

CENTRALIZATION VERSUS DECENTRALIZATION

There has been much debate about whether data processing should be centralized or decentralized. Given the right tools, it should be both. Strategic planning, corporate-wide network design, and data administration should be centralized; however, the building of individual systems needs to be as close to the end users as possible because only the users understand their real problems. Making the encyclopedia available on-line to both planners and implementers makes it practical to combine centralized planning with decentralized implementation. The IE encyclopedia is administered centrally—an extension of data administration—and it is used decentrally as systems are designed and built. The existence of the centrally controlled encyclopedia makes decentral development controllable. The advantages of development at end-user sites can occur without the spread of incompatible systems (Fig. 5.9).

MIGRATION FROM OLD SYSTEMS

When information engineering is adopted throughout an enterprise, data models and process models are created. Systems employ these models and the enterprise reaps benefits such as the following:

- Systems are integrated.
- Top management can obtain the information it needs.
- Data processing expenditure is harnessed to corporate goals.

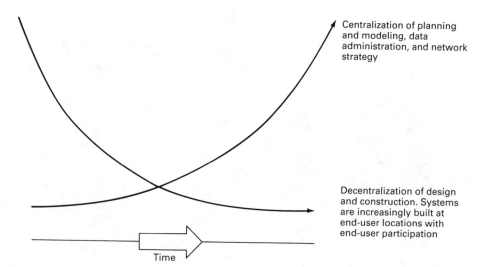

Centralization of planning and modeling, data administration, and network strategy

Decentralization of design and construction. Systems are increasingly built at end-user locations with end-user participation

Time

Figure 5.9 Decentralization of design and construction is made practical by an on-line encyclopedia with central coordination of planning, data modeling, and process modeling.

- Systems are clearly structured.
- Change is facilitated.
- The "spaghetti" of the past is replaced with clean engineering.

The systems of the past cannot all be rebuilt quickly. To do so would be too expensive and chaotic. Cleanly engineered systems are built one at a time, and they need to coexist with the old systems.

Over the years, old systems will be rebuilt. It is often less expensive to rebuild a system with CASE tools than to maintain its old code. Eventually, most old systems in an enterprise will be rebuilt so that they conform to the data models. Only then will a satisfactorily computerized enterprise exist, capable of modifying its procedures quickly to meet competitive thrusts.

Automated tools give much help in reengineering old systems. Spaghetti COBOL can be automatically converted into fully structured COBOL. The structured program then needs to be input to an I-CASE tool which first aids in converting the data to conform to the IE data models, and then enables the functionality of the program to be changed and new code generated. The screens can be changed with a screen painter. New reports can be generated. The goal should be to obtain a new system in IE format which will subsequently be inexpensive to maintain with the I-CASE design tools and code generator. The computer-aided conversion is referred to as *reverse engineering*.

Planning the migration of old systems to the IE format is an activity of business area analysis. It is often necessary to build a bridge between the old and new systems. Reverse engineering is discussed in detail in Book III.

DECAPITATION

A surprising number of I.S. executives say that they have little communication with the top management of their enterprise. Their CEO is not interested in computing. He says: "All I want to know about computers is how much they cost—and it's too much." Such computer executives comment that IE is fine but it stops at the head of I.S.; they cannot involve higher management.

Such organizations have often done an excellent job of data administration. They have often built data models and process models and have done business area analysis, at least for some business areas. They have built an IE infrastructure and gained major advantages from creating systems within that infrastructure. But the top level of the pyramid has been missing.

It is clear that this decapitated form of IE works and is very valuable. However, it misses what might be the most important advantages of IE—working with top management on how the enterprise might be restructured, what its critical success factors are and how to achieve that success, and exploring ways in which technology might make the enterprise more competitive.

REFERENCES

1. To see a JAD session functioning with a CASE tool, it is recommended that the reader and would-be JAD participants view the training tapes on JAD made by the author with ALI, 1751 West Diehl Road, Naperville, IL 60566 (312-369-3000).

2. The workshops with the bank top management are described in the tapes in Reference 1.

6 PRODUCTIVITY AND EVOLUTION

INTRODUCTION   A major objective of information engineering is to improve productivity in building computer applications. It can help improve productivity in several ways. Two of the most important are its use of automated tools and its identification of commonality of data and processes so that these need to be designed once only rather than separately for multiple applications.

In the beginning there may be a concern that IE slows down system development because it advocates that detailed data modeling and process modeling are done before design begins. IE builds a framework into which separately designed systems fit. This framework takes some time to build, but once it exists, systems can be built quickly within the framework.

In software engineering a concern about structured analysis and design is that it requires substantial work to be done before coding begins. Some implementers feel uncomfortable about delaying the code stage. They have a great urge to build something even if it is not yet designed adequately. It is only a slight exaggeration to say that many such systems are designed by testing. So little is known about the systems requirements that it is often after it is built that the truth comes to light. Structured analysis and design advocate doing more work at the front end of the life cycle and less work at the back end, especially if fourth-generation languages or code generators are used.

IE requires even more work before coding because the system must fit into the infrastructure of other systems. However, once the data models and process models exist in an IE encyclopedia, individual system design and construction can proceed rapidly if suitably automated tools are used.

I.S. PRODUCTIVITY   Many studies have been done of the effects of I.S. productivity tools, and these show major improvements in some organizations but low improvements in others using the same tools.

To achieve high productivity, it is necessary not only to select the best tools but also to adapt I.S. organization and methods to take full advantage of these tools.

The simplest CASE tools are little more than diagramming aids. They might be thought of as word processors for diagrams. (They do not have all the characteristics listed in Box 2.1.) These tools enable diagrams to be drawn more quickly and enable them to be modified quickly and kept tidy. They have a productivity effort comparable to the introduction of word processors into a lawyer's office. Lawyers' word processors often result in far more text being created; diagramming tools often result in far more diagrams being created.

A more valuable effect of good CASE tools is the removal of errors and inconsistencies at the design stage. The designs are of higher quality, leading to fewer problems and less time taken in removal of errors from code.

Code generators enable implementers to produce a working program quickly. However, if the generator is not linked to a dictionary, data model, or design tools, the programs generated may be incompatible fragments, ill designed and not linking together. To achieve high productivity, the tools for design need to be tightly coupled to the code generator. The design tools should employ a data model and should enable the design to be represented in a powerful, visual, easy-to-modify form from which code is generated directly. The programs should be quickly executable so that the designer can observe what they do, adjust or add to the design, rerun the programs, enhance the design, and so on, until a comprehensive system is created. The principle "What you see is what you get" should apply to the combination of visual design tool and code generator. The need for manual coding should be removed to the maximum extent.

The generator first produces structured code which relates to the design screens. This code may be used for prototyping and debugging. Structured code does not give optimal machine performance, so, for heavy-duty applications, the code may be fed into an optimizer which creates code with optimal machine performance. This code will never be touched by maintenance programmers.

The designer-generator tool should facilitate prototypes being built and modified quickly. It should generate test data and provide testing tools. It should generate database code and job control code, so that the program can be quickly executed when design changes are made. With powerful prototyping tools an iterative development life cycle is used. The implementer designs something on the screen of an I-CASE tool, generates code, executes the code and tests it, then modifies or adds to the design, regenerates code, and so on. The faster the cycle of design–generate–test can be (Fig. 6.1), the more productive the implementer is likely to be. Powerful design tools with interpretative generators are needed which make this cycle as fast as possible.

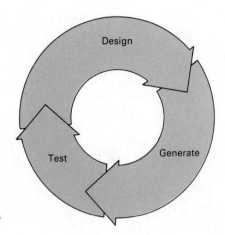

Figure 6.1

THE EFFECT OF   System development productivity is strongly affected
LARGE TEAMS   by the number of people in the system development
                       team. Large teams tend to give low development pro-
ductivity. The reason is that the number of interactions between team members
increases rapidly as team size increases. If there are N people on a team, all
interacting, the number of person-to-person interactions is $N(N-1)/2$. When people interact, there is miscommunication. The attempt to lessen miscommunication by documenting the interactions is time consuming and often does not work
well. The productivity-reducing effects are approximately proportional to the
square of the number of interacting team members.

Statistics for conventional programming show *much* larger numbers of
lines of code per person (averaged over the life of a project) for very small
teams than for large teams. Application development projects with very large
numbers of people are often disastrous. One-person projects exhibit the highest
productivity.

Figure 6.2 shows statistics for COBOL programming. The average number
of lines of code per person-year varies from 800 to 15,000, depending on the
size of the program. To a large extent this reflects the effect of large teams:
500-line programs are written by one person; 500,000 line programs are written
by large teams.

An objective of information engineering should be to avoid having large
teams. Big projects should be subdivided into small projects, each of which can
be completed relatively quickly by one, two, or, at most, three implementers
using a code generator. The CASE tool should make it possible to define with
computer precision the interfaces between the components generated by separate
teams. At the start of a large project, an entity-relationship diagram should be
created for the data that will be used; the data elements should be defined and
the data correctly normalized. The same data model should be used for all sub-

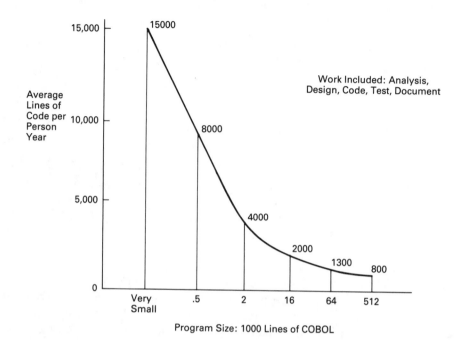

Figure 6.2 Statistics for COBOL programmers showing the large variation in number of lines per code per person-year from small to large program.

projects. The flow of data and control among subprojects should be defined with the CASE tool.

Because of the power of an I-CASE tool, many projects or subprojects can be completed by one person. The brilliant, fast, or hardworking person then has the capability of excelling. Management should encourage the most capable implementers to learn the full power of an I-CASE toolset.

VERY LARGE PROGRAMS

The implementation of very large systems—for example, systems with more than half-a-million lines of code—has often been disastrous with the process-centered techniques of software engineering. Statistics relating to COBOL indicate that most projects of this size overrun their cost and time estimates drastically, and often fail to meet the user needs. About 25 percent of such projects are canceled before completion [1].

A data-centered approach is much more successful. Even with very large projects it is relatively easy to create an entity-relationship model and normalize the data. The data on the input and output documents can be analyzed and then synthesized (with computer assistance) into a normalized data model. The large project can then be subdivided into pieces each of which delivers a usable result in its own right. The interface between the pieces is via the data model, as shown in Fig. 6.3.

The data model is built with a CASE workbench and the system is decomposed into subprocedures. The subprocedures may be linked with a data-flow diagram. The data-flow diagram, procedure decomposition diagram, and data model are linked into a hyperdiagram with computerized coordination. The subprocedures should each be a subsystem which can be implemented in its own right. Any commonality between the subprocedures, such as common screen layouts, should be designed. There is then a definition of the interface between the separately implemented pieces created with computerized precision. As separate teams build the pieces, each will build to link to the interface definition that is in the encyclopedia. The knowledge coordinator will ensure that all the pieces fit together with precision (Fig. 6.4).

A goal should be to break large projects into pieces each of which is not more than 20,000 lines of COBOL. A program of this size can normally be designed, coded, and debugged in six months by one or two implementers working with I-CASE tools.

A project of half-a-million lines of COBOL has traditionally taken 200 analysts and programmers about three years to implement. With traditional techniques it is nearly impossible to control the interfaces between 200 analysts and programmers. Using information engineering the data model for such a project can typically be created in a few weeks. The CASE decomposition into procedures can proceed in parallel with the data modeling; the procedure model and data model will be linked into a hyperdiagram. The project may be subdivided into, say, 30 or 40 pieces, each of which is implemented in six months

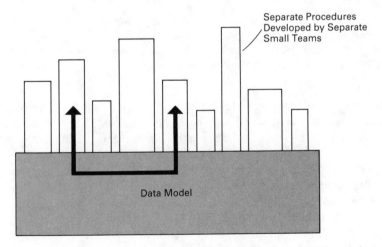

Figure 6.3   A data model can be developed quickly for a complex project. The project should be split into pieces where communication among the pieces is defined using the common data model (Fig. 6.4).

Hyperdiagram

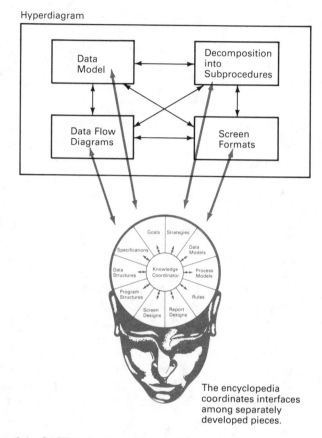

The encyclopedia
coordinates interfaces
among separately
developed pieces.

Figure 6.4 CASE tools allow a data model to be built and complex systems
subdivided into pieces which use the data model, and which can each be built
by a small team (or one person). The interfaces between the pieces is controlled on-line with computerized precision.

or less by one or two implementers. Development of many of the pieces will
go on simultaneously, but some will be done serially. The total elapsed time
may be half that with manual software engineering, and the labor requirements
much less.

Almost any data processing project can be subdivided in this way. Organizations that have used this approach comment that if you cannot subdivide a
large data processing project, you do not yet understand it well enough, and to
proceed without such understanding is to ask for trouble.

Figure 6.5 shows experience with a smaller project that would have been
about 100,000 lines of code if developed by traditional methods. It was built in
the Textile Fibers Division of DuPont using the Cortex Application Factory.
The project was split into ten projects as shown, each staffed with one, two, or

	Application	Number of Developers	Dates		Cost ($ thousands)			Application Statistics		
			Start	End	Actual	Estimated	Savings	Screens	Reports	Files
1	Passive Data	3	09/01/85	10/01/85	15.0	52.6	37.6	108	41	49
2	Production Orders	2	10/01/85	04/01/86	90.2	315.6	225.5	52	10	45
3	Time Card	2	12/01/85	02/01/86	30.1	105.2	75.2	14	3	16
4	Standard Operational Condition (SOC)	3	02/01/86	05/01/86	45.1	157.8	112.7	30	5	25
5	Product Separation	3	11/01/85	04/01/86	75.2	263.0	187.9	23	2	32
6	Process Test	2	04/01/86	08/01/86	60.1	210.4	150.3	30	2	32
7	Tracking	2	07/01/86	08/01/86	15.0	52.6	37.6	25	4	32
8	Create Product	1	01/01/96	05/01/86	60.1	210.4	150.3	31	3	55
9	System Improvement	1	07/01/86	08/01/86	15.0	52.6	37.6	10	4	8
10	Job Assignments	1	07/01/86	08/01/86	15.0	52.6	37.6	12	2	16
				Total Savings:			1053.3			

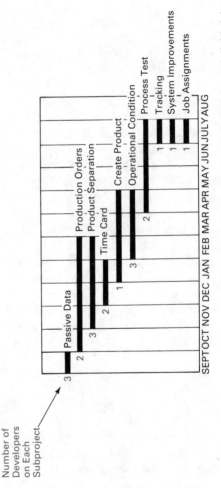

Number of Developers on Each Subproject

SEPT OCT NOV DEC JAN FEB MAR APR MAY JUN JULY AUG

Figure 6.5 Example of an information engineering project in DuPont being subdivided into pieces. With traditional techniques it would have taken about 20 person-years and an elapsed time of 2 years. It was subdivided into the ten pieces shown, each of which was implemented by one to three developers using a code generator. It took 4½ person-years and 11 months. The saving from this approach exceeded $1 million [2].

133

three developers. The dictionary-controlled code generator made possible this use of small teams working quickly.

DuPont has well-trusted estimating techniques for traditional programming. It estimated that the project would have cost $1.5 million with traditional techniques. In fact, with the techniques described, it cost $425,000 (including the costs of the software tools). More than $1 million was saved [2]. More important for DuPont, the implementation time was only 11 months and the resulting system could be maintained at low cost. Today's information engineering tools are more sophisticated than those used for this early example.

REUSABLE DESIGN AND CODE

Today's programmers constantly reinvent the wheel. They struggle to create something that has been created endless times before. Major productivity gains will result from employing reusable designs, data models, or code. Reusable components should be cataloged in a CASE encyclopedia so that they can be selected when needed and modified as required.

A large enterprise should employ the same I-CASE toolset at all locations where systems are built so that common data models, designs, and program components can be used by multiple locations. Telecommunications access to mainframe encyclopedias facilitates the sharing of applications, document design, accounting procedures, and so on.

An objective of IE is to identify commonality in both data and processes and consequently to minimize the redundant system development work. Data modeling makes it clear that the same entity types are used in numerous applications. Whenever they are used there may be certain routines that will be invoked, such as computing derived attributes, applying integrity checks, or creating summary data. A corporation may have many factories which to a large extent have the same entity types. Many of the data processing procedures can be the same from one factory to another. Some will be entirely different. The accounting and reporting should be the same in each factory so that higher-level management can make comparisons. When process decomposition is done and processes are mapped against entity types, commonality among processes can be discovered.

Westpac, one of the largest banks in the southern hemisphere, based in Sydney, used information engineering across the entire bank, with the support of its top management, who recognized that better use of computer technology was critical for the growth and success of the bank. Westpac identified 1100 processes, and each of these would probably have been programmed independently if software engineering (as opposed to IE) had been used. In practice there was so much commonality that the 1100 processes were reduced to 50, and these were designed, represented in an IE encyclopedia, and constructed with a code generator [3]. This 22:1 reduction in code generated saved much development time and is likely to reduce the maintenance effort greatly. It also helped to provide consistency of information and reporting, which is valuable to management and good for customers. I contrast this with the bank that I use, which tells me that it is "impossible" to compute net return on assets because "the computers cannot handle it." Reusable design and code ought to be a major objective of data processing development because they can dramatically reduce development and maintenance effort.

When a code generator can generate code directly from a design representation the focus of reusability is the design stage. Design modules may be stored in the encyclopedia and used when needed. The design workbench makes designs easy to modify. Being able to make adjustments to designs, and add to them as needed, greatly extends the practicality of reusable design.

Standards for application design also extend the practicality of reusable design. These include standards established in the I.S. organization for access to networks, access to databases, standard document formats, standard user dialogs, IBM's SAA (Systems Application Architecture), and so on. Common use of such standards throughout an I.S. organization equates to increases in I.S. productivity.

Book III discusses reusability techniques in more detail.

Box 6.1 summarizes measures for maximizing productivity.

BOX 6.1   How to maximize the productivity of building systems

- Use the most automated powerful design tools.
- Use design tools that catch all errors possible and catch all inconsistencies in the design.
- Use a code generator integrated with the design tool (an I-CASE tool).
- Use tools that make the cycle of design, generate, test, modify, generate, test as rapid as possible.
- Use design tools on-line to a comprehensive IE encyclopedia.
- Design within a preexisting framework of IE plan, data models, and process models.
- Use correctly normalized data models.
- Generate as much of the design from the business models and business rules as possible.
- Use IE tools that catch all inconsistencies and the data models, process models, and design.
- Use high-speed prototyping within the IE framework.
- Generate documentation automatically.

(Continued)

BOX 6.1 *(Continued)*

- Generate database code automatically.

- Employ standard screens, dialogs, and application components wherever possible.

- Employ reusable design and code wherever possible.

- Use enterprise-wide data modeling and process modeling to identify reusable modules. Store reusable models, design, and code in the IE encyclopedia.

- Employ interactive requirements planning workshops (JRP) and design workshops (JAD) with automated tools and strong participation.

- Provide all developers with a dedicated workstation linked to a central IE encyclopedia.

- Use application packages where appropriate.

- Use one-person projects where practical, where the one person has powerful workbench tools linked to the IE encyclopedia with automated enforcement of consistency and discipline.

- Use small teams, not large teams, and divide large systems into autonomous pieces that can be developed by small teams (or one person).

- Use IE techniques with automated consistency checking to divide large systems into small autonomous pieces where the interface between the pieces is rigorously defined.

- Ensure that developers have thorough training and practice with the tools.

- Measure the productivity of developers, and put the best ones on the most urgent or complex subsystems.

- Motivate the developers strongly and give major rewards for high productivity.

- Avoid interruption of developers. Create an environment in which creative developers have long periods of uninterrupted creativity.

- Use a development life cycle designed to take maximum advantage of the chosen tools—a life cycle incorporating JRP, JAD, prototyping with a user review board, fast iteration, code generation and optimization, and timebox techniques to enforce deadlines (Book III).

- Enforce consistency of the methodology used, with automated tools. Ensure that all developers and maintainers use the same tools and techniques.

EVOLUTIONARY GROWTH OF SYSTEMS

The most impressive of complex systems are not created with a single design and implementation. They evolve, being improved in many steps at different times and places.

A system designer looks at the works of nature with awe. A cheetah watching for prey at dawn suddenly races through scrub at 70 miles per hour with astonishing grace to kill a leaping antelope. A hummingbird, which engineers once "proved" was an aerodynamic impossibility, flits from flower to flower and then migrates to South America. The human brain, full of diabolical schemes and wonderful poetry, has proven far beyond our most ambitious artificial-intelligence techniques. These are not systems for which God wrote specifications; they are systems that evolved over millions of years.

The future will bring impressive software and corporate computer systems, and these will also be *grown* over many years with many people and organizations adding to them. It is difficult or impossible to *grow* software that is a mess. To achieve long-term evolution of software, we need structured models of data and structured models of processes. Designs too complex for one person to know all the details must be represented in an orderly fashion in an encyclopedia so that many people in many places can add to the design. The design needs standards and reusable components and an architecture that facilitates incremental addition of new functions. So that executives can control the behavior of computers which automatically place orders, select suppliers, make trades, and so on, the behavior should be expressible in rules and diagrams that executives understand. When development tools are designed to enable systems to evolve easily, the development life cycle truly becomes a cycle, as shown in Fig. 6.6.

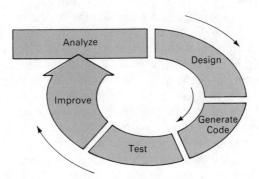

Figure 6.6 Evolutionary life cycle.

MAINTENANCE

In systems developed by traditional manual techniques, maintenance is a major problem. Systems are often difficult and time consuming to change. After being modified several times, they often become fragile and even minor changes result in bugs and breakdowns.

A goal of I-CASE toolsets is to produce systems that are quick and easy to change. Maintenance is not done by digging around in spaghetti code but by modification of the design screens, followed by regeneration of code. Thus changes can be made simply and quickly.

Traditional maintenance is often made more difficult by inadequate documentation. When maintenance programmers make changes, they often neglect to make corresponding changes to the documentation. The documentation then no longer reflects the program. With I-CASE tools, the contents of the encyclopedia *are* the documentation. Paper documentation can be generated from the encyclopedia when required. When changes are made to the design, the encyclopedia is updated automatically.

The use of I-CASE tools prevents making the spaghetti-like mess of the past and produces cleanly structured engineering with relatively fast and easy techniques for maintenance. The existing systems in most enterprises have large quantities of old code, most of which was hand built in an unstructured fashion. Their data has usually not been modeled, and little or no attempt has been made to achieve data compatibility between different systems. As well as *file systems,* there are often old *database systems* designed before today's principles of good database design were understood. The data are unnormalized and unrelated to the data administration process. Many of these old systems are fragile and expensive to maintain.

Traditional maintenance of programs is an unsatisfactory and expensive process. It has been likened to attempting to repair a wooden boat while it is at sea. New planks can be replaced only by using existing planks for support. The process must be done in small steps; otherwise, the boat will sink. After much maintenance of this type has been done, the boat becomes fragile. Attempts to change its design at sea are frustrated because no plans accurately reflect its current design. Sooner or later, the boat must be brought to a shipyard and rebuilt.

Old systems need to be rebuilt using I-CASE tools, the encyclopedia, and information engineering principles. They cannot all be rebuilt quickly because this would involve too much work. The best that can be hoped for is a steady, one-at-a-time *migration* of the old systems into the cleanly engineered form.

In corporations that have successfully implemented I-CASE methodologies, there are two development worlds. The I-CASE world has the ability to evolve systems, constantly improving their design and regenerating code. They may evolve within an IE framework with stable data models. The systems are cleanly engineered and easy to change. However, there is also an underworld of old systems, badly structured with manual code and manual design and no data models. In many corporations, more programmers work in this underworld, maintaining bad-quality code, than work in the I-CASE world (the upper half of Fig. 6.7).

The problem is rather like the slum-clearance problem in a city. A city might have a new center, elegant architecture, a well-thought-out street plan with pedestrian malls and parks, but still have large, abominable areas of slums

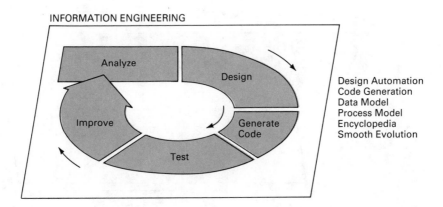

INFORMATION ENGINEERING

Design Automation
Code Generation
Data Model
Process Model
Encyclopedia
Smooth Evolution

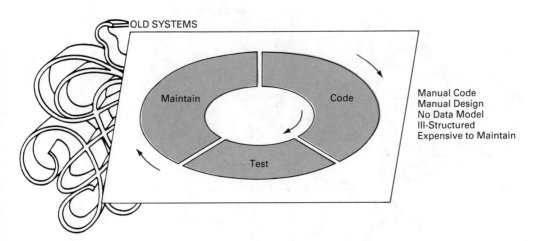

OLD SYSTEMS

Manual Code
Manual Design
No Data Model
Ill-Structured
Expensive to Maintain

Figure 6.7   Two worlds of systems development.

and old, decrepit buildings. There is no easy solution to the slum-clearance problem. The best that can be hoped for is a steady migration from the slums and their replacement with well-planned facilities.

REVERSE ENGINEERING

The costs of maintenance in the non-I-CASE world get ever higher. One of America's best telephone switches ran into so many software maintenance difficulties that its cost of maintenance exceeded $1 million *per day*. The switch would never have been built if that figure could have been forecast. A study by the U.S. Air Force estimated that if maintenance productivity cannot be changed, by A.D. 2000 it will require one-fourth of the draft-age population of the United States to maintain its software [4]!

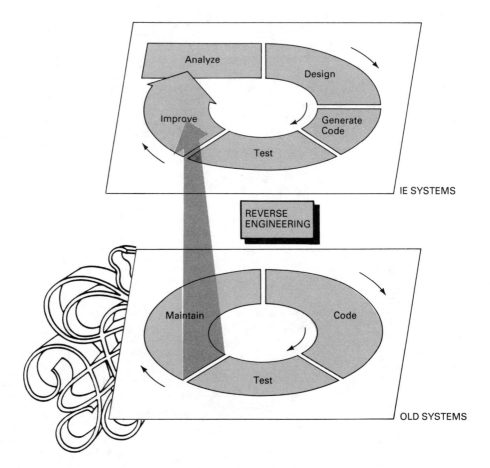

Figure 6.8   Reverse engineering step.

Fortunately, new toolsets are becoming available to facilitate the complex process of rebuilding systems. The old system is *reverse-engineered* into a cleanly structured form, using tools that automate the tedious parts of this process. The new structure is adapted so that it uses the IE data models. The programs are captured and represented in a CASE format so that they can then be modified as required using CASE tools.

Figure 6.8 shows a reverse engineering step. The code of the old system is restructured with an automated tool and entered into an I-CASE tool so that it can be analyzed and redesigned and become part of the I-CASE evolutionary life cycle. In connection with this reverse-engineering step, three terms are used and are defined as follows:

- *Restructuring:* conversion (with an automated tool) of unstructured code into fully structured code

- *Reverse engineering:* conversion of unstructured code into structured code and entry (automatic) of this into an I-CASE tool with which it can be improved or redesigned

- *Reengineering:* modification of the design of a system, adding functionality where required, and (automated) production of code for the improved system

If reverse engineering is done as shown in Fig. 6.8, old systems can be rebuilt as evolutionary systems in the upper part of the diagram. Eventually, the messy underworld of Fig. 6.8 should disappear.

REFERENCES

1. Statistics from T. Capers Jones.

2. Details from Scott Schultz, Textile Fibers Division, DuPont, Wainsborough, PA.

3. Peter Horbiatiuck, presentation to KnowledgeWare users conference, Atlanta, GA, Feb. 1988.

4. From a paper by Eric Bush, *A CASE for Existing Systems,* Language Technology Inc., Salem, MA, 1988.

7 HOW DO YOU JUSTIFY THE EXPENDITURE ON INFORMATION ENGINEERING?

INTRODUCTION Acquiring a set of information engineering tools is expensive. The I.S. executive or champion of information engineering needs to be able to justify this expenditure.

Sometimes more serious, information engineering is a disruption in the procedures and organization of I.S. Some I.S. staff resent and resist this disruption. Some I.S. managers have the attitude that it is too difficult to make information engineering work because of the human cooperation needed. High management needs to perceive clearly the financial benefits that are sought in the move to information engineering.

All organizations that are now using *software engineering* techniques as opposed to *information engineering* need to determine whether they should change. They should evaluate the costs and potential benefits of information engineering.

A concern about information engineering is that while the I.S. organization is under pressure to build new systems quickly, the planning and modeling phases of information engineering (ISP and BAA) take time and resources but do not immediately contribute to building today's systems. The benefits are long term, so they need to be understood and quantified.

As this chapter indicates, there can be a major payoff in a corporation which gets the whole act together. Most corporations have put only a part of the act into operation as yet. The big payoff comes from full integration of IE techniques, and corporations should drive for this objective.

To convince high management to spend money on long-term benefits, it is desirable to create a business plan, much as an entrepreneurial company creates a business plan in order to obtain an investment from venture capitalists. Venture capitalists do not expect immediate payback from their investment, but expect that the long-term net return on investment will be higher than other investments to justify the risks involved. The justification of information engineering needs estimates of the long-term net return on investment.

Shared data models and process models form the infrastructure of information engineering. A separate investment program is generally needed to fund the building of these since they are not part of any one user area and may not provide an adequate return on investment to any one user area by itself.

LONG-TERM INVESTMENT   Before information engineering is established, project managers or analysts may regard the planning and modeling phases as being too time consuming. It typically takes six months to do an ISP study and six months to do a business area analysis. Multiple BAAs are needed for the different business areas, and two or three years may elapse before a complete set of data models and process models exist for the enterprise.

In an organization with no data administration, an appealing dream is that the development of new systems could be put on hold while corporate data models and process models are established. In reality this is entirely impractical. New systems are being developed while the data models are evolving. Models for the new systems can be created quickly as part of their development, but they may become incompatible with the eventual corporate data models. To lessen this problem the data for the new systems should be fully normalized so that they can be converted easily to new fully normalized data models when necessary. Before cutover the new systems should be made as compatible as possible with the emerging corporate data models and process models.

FOUR TYPES OF BENEFITS   The planning and modeling stages of the IE pyramid are a long-term investment, but this should not delay the achievement of benefits from IE. The IE techniques which improve the design and construction of systems (Book III) should be applied immediately where new systems are needed, even though the IE infrastructure is not yet complete. These systems should be designed so that they can quickly be retrofitted to the data models and process models as they evolve. Also, the strategic planning stage should be used to identify information needed by decision makers and obtain it for them as quickly as practical before the detailed data models are built.

There are multiple areas of benefits from information engineering:

1. *I.S. productivity cost savings from the use of automated tools for the design and construction of systems.* Major productivity improvements can be obtained before the enterprise data models and process models are complete.

2. *Faster development.* The development cycle time has been cut to a fifth in some well-managed installations. This reduction does not occur on the first projects, but when the team becomes experienced. Often the reduction in cycle time is more important than cost savings.

3. *Management benefits that result from recognizing information needs and filling these needs quickly.*

4. *Lower maintenance costs.* Maintenance costs for systems built and modified with IE tools have been a fifth to a tenth of equivalent costs for old systems.

5. *Benefits that result from the enterprise data models and process models.* These benefits include better integration of systems, improved ability to get good information to decision makers, less complexity of information movement (as illustrated in Figs. 3.2 and 3.3), lower development costs because of preexisting data definitions, lower maintenance costs, and less development because of reusable code.

6. *Business benefits that result from recognizing strategic systems opportunities and building systems that enhance competitive thrusts or facilitate enterprise reorganization.*

The first three of these classes of benefits above can be obtained relatively quickly. The second three classes have a long-term payoff. The benefits are summarized in Box 7.1.

ESTIMATES OF FINANCIAL PAYOFF

It is possible to estimate a financial payoff for some of the items in Box 7.1. Unfortunately, items that may be the most important in Box 7.1 are impossible to quantify in advance: for example, the payoff from possible restructuring of the enterprise, or identification of strategic systems opportunities which give a major competitive advantage.

Since the dawn of the computer age it has been necessary to justify expenditure on certain systems with a large component of faith. I spent many years with IBM salespeople impressed by their ability to mix tangible estimates of return with intangible statements of opportunities. Tangible dollar estimates are almost always enough to justify IE, but the true payoff may be larger than the tangible estimates.

The items to which a financial estimate may be attached are as follows:

Savings in Design and Construction Costs

In Chapter 6 we gave illustrations of major improvements in I.S. productivity. The DuPont example was developed at less than a third of what it would have cost with traditional techniques. The best of today's IE toolkits with an integrated code generator *often do better than this*. Conservatively, it might be estimated that the use of an IE toolkit will halve the cost of design and code generation. These savings are attainable before enterprise data modeling and process modeling have been completed. The payoff can be attained in the first year of using the tools.

BOX 7.1 The payoff from information engineering

Short-Term Payoff

- Management needs for information are identified and fulfilled rapidly where possible, for example with executive information systems (Book III) or spreadsheet software.

- Attention is focused in an organized fashion on goals, problems, and critical success factors. Some immediate actions can be taken relating to these. Critical success factor measures are monitored. That which is monitored tends to improve.

- Certain information systems can be built quickly, using power tools, within the IE framework.

- Productivity tools and techniques enable systems to be designed and implemented more quickly, before data modeling and process modeling of the enterprise is completed.

Long-Term Payoff

- Strategic uses of technology are identified, leading to the building of strategic information systems. This may have a very high payoff.

- Management understanding of the enterprise is improved, often leading to enterprise reorganization. This is also important but impossible to quantify in advance.

- The same data is represented in the same way in different systems, leading to integration among systems where needed. Without this integration some important information needs cannot be met. IE avoids a Tower of Babel in computerized data.

- Common usage of database systems leads to simpler, less expensive data flows (Figs. 3.2 and 3.3).

- Major savings are made possible through reusable design and code.

- Designing and constructing systems with a workbench and code generator using the IE encyclopedia enables systems to be built much faster and less expensively.

- The costs of maintenance are lowered dramatically.

- Systems can be built quickly when they are needed by the enterprise, partly because of faster development methods (Book III) and partly because the backlog is reduced. There are major business benefits from fast development when it is needed, such as fast response to competitive pressures and the building of strategic systems before competition has them. them.

- An evolutionary life cycle is supported in which systems can steadily grow in comprehensiveness, becoming uniquely valuable to the enterprise.

Faster Development Cycle Time

A goal of usage of the IEF (Information Engineering Facility) in Texas Instruments is to cut the development cycle time to one fifth. This 5 to 1 reduction has been achieved on some projects but only after the developers and manager have built up the requisite skill, methodology, and experience.

Productivity Improvements Due to Existence of Data Models

When data models exist and new systems are built with these data models, further time and cost will be saved in designing systems. In traditional application development with COBOL it has been found that the use of preexisting databases reduces programming time by 20 to 40 percent [1]. Use of database fourth-generation languages, where appropriate, gives further reduction. Many small applications can be created quickly with report generators.

Savings Due to Commonality of Data— Avoiding a Tower of Babel with Data

In the nonintegrated environment illustrated by Fig. 3.2, much communication of data is done by paperwork, which is error prone, time consuming, and labor intensive. The passing of information among separate systems requires that the information be converted. Changes made to one system can play havoc with others. Often, passing information between incompatible systems involves complex procedures. To prevent the harmful effects of change, the management procedures become rigid and change is made difficult.

In the integrated environment of Fig. 3.3 the data flows are greatly simplified. Procedures are simpler. Fewer people are involved. The data is consistent and more likely to be accurate. This has two effects: the streamlining of business procedures and the simplification of programs.

The simplification of procedures and programs is a longer-term payoff of information engineering. It may be achieved two years or so after business area analysis has been done for the area in question. How easily it can be done depends to some extent on how automated is the reengineering of systems (Book III).

Reduction in Maintenance Costs

When systems are created with I-CASE tools using a powerful code generator, these systems cost much less to maintain. Maintenance is done by regeneration rather than by modifying COBOL code. When systems are streamlined, use a common data model, and use databases from which reports can be quickly generated, less maintenance effort is needed. Reduction in maintenance cost is a long-term payoff of information engineering. It may be conservative to estimate a halving of maintenance expenditure. In practice, a 10 to 1 reduction has been achieved in some systems built and maintained with a tool that has a powerful code generator.

Savings Due to Reusable Design and Code

A goal of process modeling is to identify common processes. When object-oriented database techniques are used, processes are associated with a database entity type (object type). Multiple types of transactions using that entity type may invoke the same process.

We commented that information engineering at the Westpac Bank in Australia resulted in 50 processes being used, whereas 1100 would have been needed if software engineering had been done with isolated projects. This is a dramatic example of savings due to reusable design and code. It would normally be appropriate to estimate a lower proportion of reusable code, however, substantial savings in the cost of I.S. development and maintenance can accrue from reusability.

Business Benefits from Better Integrated Systems

The streamlining of administrative procedures (as illustrated by Figs. 3.2 and 3.3, for example) saves staff costs. An estimate might be made of this long-term payoff. In addition to staff savings there may be savings in other resources. For example, one organization had many inventory locations stocking the same types of items. Process modeling indicated that much of this redundancy was unnecessary. Multiple inventory locations were eliminated and procedures were established for combined inventory control which lowered the overall quantity (and cost) of inventory held.

Process modeling has often enabled results to be achieved with fewer administrative procedures. In addition to saving work and staff, results are obtained more quickly and with less overhead.

Integrated design can help to achieve *just-in-time inventory control,* in which goods arrive at a location when they are needed and do not have to sit (expensively) in inventories longer than necessary.

Business Benefits from Better Information

A goal of information engineering is to get the right information to the right people at the right time. Can the benefits from this be quantified?

Texas Instruments established an information center operation in 1983 and measured its annualized benefits as carefully as they could. Five years after initiation its measured benefits were 1.6 percent of TI's gross revenue, and these financial benefits were steadily growing worldwide [2]. This percentage seems achievable in other organizations also. Much of it relates to end-user employment of tools rather than to information engineering alone. It is desirable to combine getting the right information to the right people with making them skilled at using spreadsheet tools, report generators, graphics tools, decision-support tools, and communication facilities. The benefits from developing excellent databases for end users might be assessed independently of the benefits from spreadsheets, and so on, as, say, 0.5 percent of gross revenue, if end users everywhere were trained to use the databases.

Identification of Strategic Business Opportunities

The identification and building of strategic systems that make a business more competitive may override the other benefits of IE in its financial effect. One aspect of this is the ability to change procedures quickly when such change is desirable. No reliable estimate can be made of what this will add to the earnings. A target might be set which is to improve current earnings by, say, 10 percent, depending on circumstances.

Damage from Badly Engineered Systems

A financial justification for evolving to IE should include estimates of the harmful effects of bad engineering of data and procedures.

Just prior to the era of I-CASE development, Bank of America attempted to replace an aged computer system that managed $34 billion in institutional trust accounts. The new system was intended to attract more business. The system proved difficult to shake down, was late, and crashed when finally cut over. A *Business Week* article stated that, because of this, big pension funds pulled out at least *$1.5 billion* [3]. Vice-presidents in charge of technology and the trust divi. 'on resigned. Eventually Bank of America abandoned the code and set up a $60 million fund to correct the difficulties.

Problems on an even grander scale have occurred in the Department of Defense. A top-of-the-front-page article in the Washington Post said that the Air Force logistics system could support a war for no longer than three weeks because of software problems. Procurement of an important over-the-horizon radar system was cancelled because of software [3].

The Bank of America system had 2½ million lines of COBOL when it was abandoned. Any system of this size should be split into many separate pieces which can be implemented by relatively small teams with a code generator. To ensure that the separate pieces fit together a normalized data should be completed before detailed design is done. It is relatively easy to synthesize a normalized data model even on the largest of projects. The splitting into pieces should be done with an I-CASE tool which integrates the data model with the decomposition diagrams, data-flow diagrams, dialog and report design, and action diagrams. Complete integrity among these diagrams, for all pieces of the system, should be enforced rigorously with an IE knowledge coordinator. The computerized design should feed a code generator, database generator, and documentation generator. Detailed design calculations should be done as the design evolves to ensure that the hardware capacity is large enough.

There is a world of difference between the Bank of America experience and that of Westpac, Australia, which used information engineering across the entire bank with an integrated encyclopedia and a code generator [4].

One effect on business of non-automated software development which is particularly harmful is the inability to change procedures quickly and to create new procedures quickly.

A *Software News* survey in 1987 reported that large corporations (revenue > \$5 billion) had a mainframe development backlog of 50.75 months, medium-sized corporations (revenue between \$1 billion and \$5 billion) had a mainframe backlog of 61.45 months, and corporations with revenue below \$1 billion, 36.25 months [5]. The business effect of such backlogs is severe, and in reality the situation is worse than these numbers imply because there is an invisible backlog. Many end users do not ask for computerized procedures when they need them because they can see no point, as the delay is too great. A survey done by the Sloane Business School found the invisible application backlog in typical Fortune 500 corporations to be 168 percent of the recorded application backlog on average [6].

Even if a high-priority application jumps the backlog queue, it is likely to take two or more years to build with traditional techniques. In a mature IE environment the data for the new procedures is usually in place. Reports can be generated from this data quickly and new procedures created relatively quickly with code generators.

There are numerous examples of failure to modify computerized procedures leading to competitive disadvantage and loss of business. A confidential report on the U.S. insurance industry was written about the threat of Japanese invasion of U.S. markets by means of a large on-line sales-and-service system. It concluded:

> A group of companies appear to have lost momentum in their systems development efforts to support their core insurance business. Their systems have fallen into such a state of disrepair that they are consumed with the effort to provide quick fixes. They are the most vulnerable of the major companies to a Japanese invasion.
>
> Other systems organisations including Company X, Company Y and Company Z, are to some degree demoralized and treading water. Company Z has been heavily focused on short term fixes.
>
> Other companies have been caught in the whiplash of changing strategic thrusts, neglect of support for core insurance business, decentralization of application development or arbitrary down sizing. Their ''old hands'' are

weary and cynical. Their systems efforts are not based on a business vision, nor on integrated systems to restructure processes, but instead on a bottom-up mongolian-horde design approach.

These companies are vulnerable to competitive threats from abroad, from the next generation of technology-based sales-and-service systems, and from the effective niche players.

Such comments would apply to other industries also. There is a major business need to replace messy computing and messy data with cleanly engineered systems designed for ease of change.

The following two quotes are typical of the non-IE environment [7]:

DP Executive:

The business was slipping out of control. There was no correlation between the different systems. There were 260 files all with financial information updated at different times. There had been major errors in assessing the overall cash position. And the situation was rapidly getting worse.

Systems Analyst:

Large customers could not tell how much money they had in the bank. They have many time deposits all coming due at different times, on-call deposits, numerous different account numbers for the same customer. No one statement contained more than a portion of the customer's cash position. All the data was on-line but we couldn't tie it together. Incidentally some of it was in database form but it had been designed like a collection of separate systems with no integration. The thing that finally put the management heat on it was two big customers moved to a different bank with better account management.

A goal of IE is to achieve better control of data than is possible with separately designed data. In some organizations the worsening proliferation of incompatible data takes them dangerously close to chaos.

AN EXAMPLE OF IE JUSTIFICATION   Let us consider the costs of IE in a corporation with a gross revenue of $1 billion. This corporation has a total I.S. expenditure of $50 million, including its telecommunications and office automation expenditures. Its development backlog is three years and it has a large invisible backlog. The total I.S. staff is 270 people, of whom 170 work on maintenance and enhancement of existing systems. Figure 7.1 shows the current expenditures, the estimated expenditures on IE, and the estimated benefits from IE.

It is assumed that all software and workbench computers are purchased.

Current Revenue and I.S. Costs

Gross revenue	1,000,000
Total I.S. expenditure (including telecommunications and office automation)	50,000
Total I.S. staff and support: 260 people	20,000
Total I.S. staff working on maintenance and enhancement: 170 people	12,000
Current mainframe backlog: 3 years (not including large invisible backlog)	

Estimated Cost of Information Engineering

	Year 1	Year 2	Year 3	Year 4	Year 5
• Staff doing ISP	300	50	50	50	50
• Staff doing BAA	300	600	600	200	150
• Tools for ISP and BAA	200	50	50	50	50
• Tools for design and coding	800	800	600	400	400
• Training costs	120	200	100	50	50
• Consulting costs	200	100	—	—	—
	1920	1800	1400	750	700

I.S. Benefits from Information Engineering

• Increased productivity in system design and construction					
i. Due to automated tools	500	2000	3000	3000	3000
ii. Due to existence of data models		500	1000	1000	1000
iii. Due to reusable design and code			2000	3000	3000
• Reduction in maintenance costs			2000	4000	6000
	500	2500	8000	11000	13000

Figure 7.1 Illustration of the justification of a move to information engineering in a $1 billion corporation. (All figures are in thousands of dollars.)

(Continued)

Business Benefits from Information Engineering

	Year 1	Year 2	Year 3	Year 4	Year 5
● Administrative savings from better-integrated systems			500	1000	2000
● Business benefits from better-quality systems			500	1000	1000
● Business benefits from better information to end users	200	1000	2000	3000	4000
● Business benefits from faster development of procedures	200	500	1000	2000	2000
● Benefits from strategic business opportunities (these might be much higher)		500	2000	4000	4000
	400	2000	6000	11000	13000
Net benefits (loss)	(1020)	2700	12600	21250	25300
Percent of current gross revenue	(0.1%)	0.3%	1.3%	2.1%	2.5%

Figure 7.1   (Continued)

Most of the expenditure for tools therefore occurs in years 1 and 2. There are also training and consulting costs in years 1 and 2. To offset the startup costs, there is an emphasis on obtaining benefits *quickly* by identifying important management information needs and responding to them, and by using automated design and coding extensively before the corporate data modeling and process modeling are completed. There are business benefits from better information and faster development in the first year.

The reduction in system development costs due to data models and reusable design and code are substantial but take some time to achieve. The reduction in maintenance costs is larger and takes even longer to achieve.

Mr. John White, the I.S. executive at Texas Instruments, states that in projects with mature, experienced use of IE a 5:1 reduction is achieved in the total development cycle time, and a 10:1 reduction in maintenance effort occurs when maintaining a system developed with full IE automation, compared to a system built with non-automated design and programming. The 5:1 reduction is not achieved on the first projects tackled; it depends on the team and its manager having experience with the IE toolset and methodology [8]. The estimate in Fig. 7.1 is that maintenance costs are halved by the end of year 5.

Substantial reengineering of old systems has been done to achieve this. An evolutionary life cycle is emphasized in which systems can be modified and added to quickly and easily by changing design screens and regenerating code.

The corporation steadily acquires *better quality* systems and *better integrated* systems. The benefits of this are shown as starting to build up in year 3. One of the benefits is simpler administrative procedures and fewer staff.

As mentioned, the measured benefits from the information center operations in Texas Instruments became 1.6 percent of gross revenue in year 5. This would be equivalent to $16 million in Fig. 7.1 (or more if revenue increased). Benefits of $4 million are shown as accruing from information engineering in conjunction with end-user computing.

A major effect of information engineering is faster development and modification of procedures. In some organizations the business effect of this has been substantial. It becomes larger in the fourth and fifth years because the data models are complete and some old systems have been reengineered by then. It is difficult to estimate the business benefits quantitatively.

Still more difficult to estimate are the benefits from identifying and building strategic or mission-critical systems. The best examples of such systems have had a major impact on corporate growth and profits. The estimate in Fig. 7.1 is 0.4 percent of gross revenue, and it may be possible to do much better than this.

There is much uncertainty in estimates of business effects such as those in Fig. 7.1, as indeed there are in most business plans requesting venture capital. A venture capitalist monitors his investment to try and make the estimated benefits achievable. Similarly, the progress of information engineering should be monitored from the business point of view to try to maximize its benefits. Where benefits a fraction of those in Fig. 7.1 can be achieved, no enterprise of any size can afford *not* to do information engineering.

REFERENCES

1. Statistics collected by T. Caper Jones.

2. From charts of a presentation of the TI Information Center, provided by Mr. John White, TI's head of I.S., 1987.

3. *Business Week*, The Software Trap: Automate—or Else, May 8, 1988.

4. Detailed description from Peter Horbietuik, Westpac, Sydney.

5. *Software News,* Survey on Application Development, Nov. 1987.

6. R. B. Rosenbury, The Information Center, *SHARE 56,* Proceedings of Session M372, Share Inc., New York, 1981.

7. From interviews in the video series "Managing the Data Base Environment," made with James Martin, Advanced Learning International, Naperville, IL.

8. John White, speech to Women in Computing Conference, Dallas, Sept. 21, 1988.

8 THE CORPORATION OF THE FUTURE

INTRODUCTION   The corporation of the future will be a highly computerized enterprise, its competitiveness and its survival depends on how effectively it uses automation.

Computers are changing the fabrication techniques and changing the products because products can have elaborate computation facilities built into them—a modern camera contains 150,000 transistors. Networks are changing the flows of information and the interactions between far-flung parts of the enterprise. Information can flow worldwide in seconds. Worldwide data can be made available on anyone's desk, with tools for processing the data. Computerized expertise will be available to decision makers and professionals.

The corporate data network, like the nervous system of a creature, will go to every part of the organism. Networks will link suppliers directly to producers and producers to their customers. Computers in one organization will send information directly to computers in another organization. Knowledge workers with easy-to-use workstations will be able to interrogate databases anywhere. The vast infrastructure built for an obsolete world of paper shuffling will no longer be needed.

Innovative companies are perceiving how computers, networks, artificial intelligence, workstations, CD-ROMs, and other technology can enable them to launch preemptive marketplace attacks. It is clear that *most* corporations are still far from perceiving or capitalizing on the opportunities that information technology offers from maximizing their profits or market share. As technology increases the opportunities and competitive threats, so it becomes increasingly vital for the CEO to work with his top computer executives to identify the new opportunities and how technology can best be put to work. The MIS executive who talks the language of top management and who can identify and categorize the opportunities is a valuable asset. The salaries of such executives have risen greatly as information technology has become perceived as a strategic weapon rather than merely a support tool.

WHERE SHOULD DECISIONS BE MADE?

Given the ability to put a workstation on *anyone's* desk which can access databases anywhere, extract data, and do local computations with that data, the question arises: Where should decisions best be made? Information about any operations can be brought to the desk of *any* decision maker; the worldwide logistics can be made visible in the head office. Any decision maker can have access to great computer power and powerful decision-support software.

Certain types of decisions ought to be made locally, as close to the problem as possible. Decisions about shop floor loading and routing should be made *on the shop floor*. Other types of decisions should be made centrally where the worldwide operations can be viewed. Central decisions may be made about production planning, crew scheduling in an airline, inventory control with parts that can be flown around the world, currency control, and financial planning.

Many examples exist of decision making moving from distributed locations to a central location once the necessary information can be transmitted electronically. Many other examples exist of a skill that was developed centrally being moved to local operations. There are cases of head office executives interfering in decisions that were best made locally. Many other cases exist of top management and their staff not having the information they need for effective control.

Information engineering gives the capability to get the right information to the right people at the right time, and to give them tools for processing it. When that capability exists there are subtle questions about who is best suited to make what decisions. The management structure of the fully computerized corporation should be quite different from that of its predecessor with batch processing.

The enterprise model showing the functional decomposition, organization chart, geographical structure, goals, and hierarchy of critical success factors is essential in thinking about who needs what information and who should be making what types of decisions.

FLATTENING THE BUREAUCRATIC TREE

With networks able to deliver information to the desk of anyone who needs it, there is less need for organization structures many layers deep. Decisions tend to be made either at the bottom of the tree close to the problem, or at the top of the tree where integrated planning is possible. The effect of powerful decision-support software, expert systems, and information engineering is to enable a person to have a greater span of control over events. He needs fewer staff assistants. He can manage more with today's computers than he could without them.

New organizations built to take advantage of modern computing have wider, shallower organization charts than their paper-intensive predecessors. The vast office areas with stacked in-baskets are replaced with electronics. Data

flows directly from the bottom of the organization chart, where staff interact
with customers or production processes, to the top, where planning and control
is done. Some new, highly automated car plants, for example, have a leaner,
flatter, less bureaucratic management structure than that of the older car plants
in Detroit. Figure 8.1 illustrates the flattening of the bureaucratic tree as data
networks facilitate new flows of information.

Many organizations have reshaped their managerial structure around the
flow of information that computer networks make possible. In some this has
been done on a worldwide basis. Some Japanese trading companies have
adapted their management structure to take advantage of worldwide networks.
Worldwide information can now be instantly available to decision makers in a

Computer Networks Cause
Restructuring of
Business

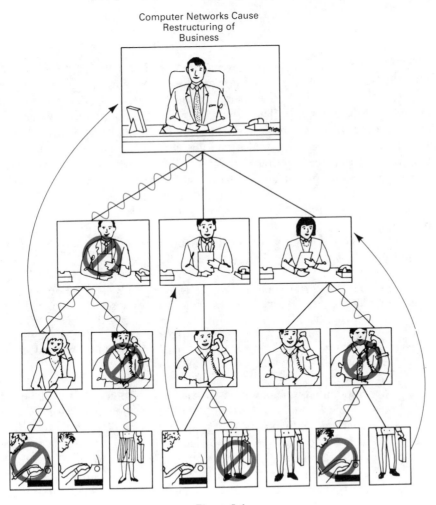

Figure 8.1

head-office location. Some organizations have reorganized the locations at which they have inventories as central knowledge of all inventories was analyzed by computer and showed how the total world inventory could be reduced. Corporations implementing computer-integrated manufacturing have found it necessary to restructure and redesign their management as an information-based organization.

When a flatter organization chart is adopted, the executives who remain usually have more demanding, more responsible jobs. They control a higher volume of operations because they can handle more information with the computerized systems. They can span a wider area of operations because of networks. The supervisor in an automated plant controls a far higher volume of production. The financial decision maker can handle a far broader range of decisions and do more elaborate computations.

ORCHESTRA-LIKE STRUCTURE

The traditional organization has a hierarchical structure. Command flows down from the top. Information gathered at the bottom is successively summarized and passed to the top. The organization built around computer networks is often entirely different. Information passes horizontally from one operating unit to another. In principle, all information can be made available to any person at any time. In practice, this bulk of information is overwhelming and careful design must be done of what information each operating unit needs. The corporate data resides in databases that any operating unit could access. Operating units extract information which they need and restructure it for their own decision making.

Peter Drucker, the doyen of management consultants, compared the new corporate structures to a symphony orchestra:

> The conventional organization of business was originally modeled after the military. The information-based system much more closely resembles the symphony orchestra. All instruments play the same score. But each plays a different part. They play together, but they rarely play in unison. There are more violins but the first violin is not even the ''boss'' of the horns, indeed the first violin is not even the ''boss'' of the other violins. [1]

In the symphony orchestra type of enterprise some of the players are highly skilled. Some know how to use computerized tools and information access to make complex decisions or do complex design. The supervisor of the automated plant has a complex set of knowledge about how the plant works and how to control it. The information-based corporation tends to use far more ''soloists''—bright individuals doing a highly skilled task on their own. They exist in a variety of different specializations—financial analysts, marketing experts, customer service personnel, production schedulers, decision makers with their own computerized models. Drucker describes how Citibank appointed a senior vice-president, for example, in its New York headquarters to take care of the bank's major Japanese customers and their worldwide financial needs:

> This man is not the "boss" of the bank's large branches in Japan. But he is not "service" staff either. He is very definitely "line." He is a soloist and expected to function somewhat the way the pianist playing a Beethoven concerto is expected to function, and both he and the "orchestra" around him, that is the rest of the bank, can function only because both "know the score." It is information rather than authority that enables them mutually to support each other. [1]

The "score" of the well-orchestrated enterprise is the information in databases which anyone with authority can access. The knowledge in the encyclopedia for the top two pyramid layers defines this information and how it is used. It defines the objectives of each organizational unit.

In the orchestra the score is given to both players and conductor. In business the score is being written as it is being played. To know what the score is, everyone in the information-based organization has to manage by objectives that are agreed upon in advance and clearly understood. Management by objectives and self-control is, of necessity, the integrating principle of the information-based structure [1].

Without the integrated planning and design of data that are achieved by information engineering, the orchestra model of an enterprise cannot work. Common language and common representation of data are essential; otherwise, the separate players create a cacophony.

It is sometimes thought that military-like hierarchical organizations have much more discipline than is possible with more horizontal organizations. To some people the horizontally structured organization conjures up an image of loose·discipline and permissiveness. This is not the case in a successful information-based enterprise. A high level of self-control is necessary. Each organizational unit needs the other units to work well and have a common base of information, mutual understanding, and mutual respect. The Digital Equipment Corporation is a decentralized enterprise that places a high value on autonomous decision making, but it has achieved a product line much more unified than IBM, which has a military-like hierarchical structure. At DEC, autonomous organizational units, with computer networks designed to get them the information they need, can make fast decisions and give fast responses. An enterprise that consists of a network of autonomous units can be highly flexible, creative, and diverse.

The information-based organization with semiautonomous units needs a high level of discipline and an overall architecture. Each unit has to understand its objectives. Management by objectives is essential. A high value is placed on local initiative in meeting the objectives as excellently as possible. Each unit has to understand how it relates to other units, how other units can help it, and how other units depend on it. This needs architectural planning and strong decisive leadership. As Drucker comments:

> First-rate orchestra conductors are without exception unspeakably demanding perfectionists. What makes a first-rate conductor is, however, the ability to make even the most junior instruments at the last desk way back play as if the performance of the whole depended on how each one of those instruments renders its small supporting part. What the information-based organization requires, in other words, is leadership that respects performance but demands self-discipline and upward responsibilities from the first-level supervisor all the way to top management. [1]

The great corporation of the future will have highly disciplined overall leadership of many autonomous units, each doing the most excellent job it can within a framework architected by information engineering.

COMPUTER-INTEGRATED MANUFACTURING

Automation affects both physical work and information work. In some corporations robotized factories are leading to a new era of high-volume fabrication in which goods of great complexity will be mass-produced with startlingly few person-hours of work. Some robot-controlled production lines work 24 hours a day, seven days a week. Most human beings work only during the prime shift and prepare what the machines will need for the night shifts.

A factory in IBM was upgraded from manufacturing 3278 terminals to 3178 terminals. A robot-operated production line was introduced. Before the change 700 terminals per day were produced by 130 people. After the change 2000 per day were produced by five people. Productivity in terms of numbers of products per person per day went from 5.4 to 400, a 7400 percent improvement in productivity. With the same reorganization the inventory turnover fell from five times per year to 80 times per year. In other words, the cost of the inventory fell from 10 weeks' supply to less than 1 week's supply. Before the change the mean time between failures of the product was one year; after the change it was eight years. This increase in reliability occurred partly because of the improvement in product design and partly because the product was made by robots, which do not make the types of mistakes that people make.

The type of organization introduced in this factory needed to be integrated with computerized order acceptance, inventory control, scheduling, planning, diagnosis of problems, shipping, and so on. This integration is referred to as CIM (computer-integrated manufacturing). There are other equally dramatic examples of robot production lines. When an automated production line is introduced, many other changes are needed to maintain the flow of work that keeps the expensive machinery busy. The attempt is made to do this with "just-in-time" inventory control. In other words, goods arrive shortly before they are needed so that inventory costs are kept low. This requires tight computerized control. Many different aspects of computerization need to be integrated.

The type of automated facility that enables IBM to produce 2000 machines per day with five people can be applied to the production of vacuum cleaners, hi-fi units, digital television sets, cameras, intelligent cookers, and all manner of other goods. The world is on the brink of a quantum leap in automated fabrication. All manner of goods, with highly elaborate built-in-microelectronics, will be mass-produced in great quantity for low prices.

However, while IBM succeeded in achieving such a dramatic change in productivity with CIM, many factories are far from it. Some have as little chance of achieving it as a hang-glider pilot has of crossing the ocean. As the most efficient corporations automate, it is difficult to see how the least efficient ones can stay in business. As with most major advances in technology, CIM will cause a major shakeout.

The factors that make CIM difficult is implied in its middle initial. Many different aspects of computerization have to be *integrated* to build today's factory automation. This aspect of complex integration applies not only to factories but also to distribution channels, bank networks, insurance companies, military logistics, airline operations, and so on. We are moving into an era when many complex aspects of computing have to work together. The future of computing is a battle with complexity.

On-line ordering and tracking of orders is necessary to minimize inventories or achieve just-in-time inventory control. Inland Steel provides services to customers which enables them to track orders of steel, and estimates that the customer's saving in inventory costs from this are greater than the difference between American and Japanese steel prices.

AUTOMATED LINKS BETWEEN CORPORATIONS When a computer generates a purchase order this should not be printed, mailed, and keypunched, but rather transmitted electronically to the vendor computer. Keypunching is tedious, error-prone work, and systems will be designed to avoid it where possible. In order to do this, the appropriate data formats need to be agreed among corporations, or better, industry standard data formats should be used. The U.S. National Bureau of Standards and the United Nations have created standards for documents exchanged electronically among businesses, such as purchase orders and invoices. The Department of Defense ICAM project has standard formats for the CAD representation of parts. Any standards that facilitate electronic exchange among corporations should be well publicized.

Corporations with many factories or worldwide operations should do all of their intercorporate ordering and billing using their own standard data formats.

These formats need to reside in the data models at each location. A central planning organization should have its own encyclopedia for representing corporate-wide flows of information and data formats. Segments of this central encyclopedia should be copied onto the encyclopedia of the individual corporations in the group or individual business units.

The searching of catalogs and the placing of orders from a catalog should take place at workstation screens where possible. This helps the person doing the ordering and avoids the clumsy interim stages of writing, mailing, and keypunching. Many corporations are providing customers or agents with terminals for placing orders, tracking the status of orders, searching catalogs, and so on. American Airlines gained great competitive advantage by placing such terminals in the offices of travel agents. Even though the terminals gave information about the flights of other airlines, they increased the probability that the agent would book American Airlines' seats rather than those of competing airlines. If the agent books a seat on another airline, American collects a service fee. It is estimated that American increased its bookings by 15 to 20 percent with this system. The pretax profit from the system is estimated to exceed $150 million a year.

Workstations in one corporation, on-line to another corporation, sometimes provide complex services. Insurance companies provide agents with systems that enable them to make complex decisions about contracts and renewals. Some companies allow customers access to their database to track their orders and shipments. Sometimes customers can configure products on-line, examining and pricing many complex alternatives. In some cases financial or administration services are provided to small agencies. Some agencies worldwide are on-line to corporations whose products they market. The world of the future will be a vast intercorporate network with the computers in each organization interacting automatically with the computers in its trading partners.

The new Saturn car plant of General Motors is designed so that many of the parts suppliers are in the same factory complex. The manufacturing schedules of the suppliers are then tightly linked to the assembly of the cars. The plant is on-line to car dealers. There are many options in configuring the car. The dealer works out with the customer what options he desires, using a computer to assemble pictures of the car with different options and to price the resulting car. The order is transmitted to the computers at the Saturn plant and manufacturing of that car can begin quickly. The car being assembled travels on an automatically guided pallette to *only* those assembly points that are needed for the order in question. The parts inventory and scheduling are adjusted accordingly. The customer can have the custom-configured car in a few days.

This level of automation requires the integration of many different computer applications—a much higher level of integration than has been used in the past. The entire complex is designed to operate without paper to the maximum extent practical. Accounting is on-line. Expense accounts, for example, are to be handled by filling in details at a screen. This further complicates the integration of the separate systems.

SHORTENING REACTION TIME

When separate organizational locations are linked by computer networks, organizational reaction times become shorter. An event in one location is immediately felt in a different location. As separate corporations become linked electronically, one can nudge the other into action at electronic speed.

A customer purchases a car and the order is immediately transmitted to the car factory and absorbed into production schedules. Events on the stock market flash to faraway machines which make, buy, or sell computations and instantly transmit these to worldwide exchanges. Clothes buyers change their buying patterns in San Francisco, and Benetton's computers in Rome take immediate action. Stationery stores minimize their inventory because they have personal computers on-line to United Stationers, which guarantees to rush orders to their customers on the day they place them.

The windows of opportunity in business are of shorter duration when corporations are linked electronically. Price advantages have to be used immediately. To achieve "just-in-time" inventory control, suppliers have to deliver exactly when computers tell them to. Electronic mail and facsimile give instant interactions. Computers generate sales proposals. The computer in one corporation scans the possible vendors electronically and orders on-line from the computer in another corporation.

The business world has speeded up because of computers, and will speed up much more when computers in one corporation are generally in electronic communication with computers in other corporations. The world will soon be a complex web of intricately interacting computers.

In such a world if an enterprise takes three years to introduce new computerized procedures, it will be at a serious disadvantage compared to enterprises that can introduce and modify procedures quickly. First Boston in New York in the turbulent financial markets of the second half of the 1980s was able to introduce new financial vehicles more quickly than its competitors because it built the computer applications with a code generator within an information engineering framework. The classical development life cycle is deadly in such an environment because it is so slow, because it fails to integrate separate systems, and because it often builds systems that do not meet the true business needs. In many cases so little is known by the programmers about the real business requirements that it is only after the system has been built that the truth comes to light.

Innovative companies are perceiving how computers, networks, workstations, and other technology can enable them to launch preemptive marketplace attacks. Computing and information systems are now strategic weapons, not a backroom overhead. As technology increases competitive opportunities and threats, the time cycle for implementing computerized procedures shrinks. It is increasingly necessary to build new applications quickly and to build them so that they can quickly be modified.

SHEEP AND GOATS

We cannot design and maintain the complex integration of systems that is needed unless we use computers themselves for this task. We need the *automation of automation*.

There is today a vast difference between the design and maintenance of computer systems in the best and worst I.S. organizations. The best are using disciplined information engineering with automated tools. The worst are using plastic templates and creating spaghetti code.

The salesperson of factory automation keeps away from the backward factories with vines covering the walls. The salesperson of design-automation tools keeps away from the I.S. departments that have not moved to structured programming and design. The best corporations upgrade to the most modern tools; the worst are left to fester in their disorganized mess.

RIGOROUS ENGINEERING

Automation directly affects productivity. Information systems directly affect decision making. Computers and networks are growing rapidly in cost-effectiveness, and increasingly in the future, corporations with poor automation and information systems will not be able to compete.

As systems become more complex they cannot sensibly be built without rigorous engineering. We cannot achieve rigorous engineering of software and information without automated tools. Tools for the design of systems must be linked to tools for code generation. Complex systems need tools that facilitate iterative or exploratory development. The tools must relate to the entire I.S. pyramid so that separately developed systems link together and strategic control of systems is practical. The tools should enforce full structuring of code and data, with automated editors so that systems are as easy to change as possible. The maintenance trap is extremely harmful; it prevents a corporation from changing its procedures to keep up with the dynamic evolution of the business. Well-engineered systems built with the most automated tools are designed so that they can be modified quickly. The tools should ensure this ease of modification.

INTEGRATION OF SYSTEMS

Separate systems are developed by separate teams. It is not practical for one team to build all the facilities of a complex corporation. To make the separately developed systems work together, techniques for synthesis and coordination are needed. A top-down overview is needed of the processes and the data that is used. The data employed by the separately developed systems must be compatible—it should be derived from the same overall data model.

By developing the separate systems using the same encyclopedia, compatibility of data can be achieved. The analysis features of the encyclopedia check that the systems link together logically. Information engineering is achieved by synthesizing the knowledge of many people, who may be scattered widely across a large enterprise. Synthesis using automated tools is essential because no single person has more than a fraction of the knowledge required. In addition to ensuring *logical* compatibility it is necessary that the systems are compatible from the *networking* point of view. Overall strategic planning of the corporate network is essential.

Knowledge of the enterprise and its systems in the IE encyclopedia grows steadily. It helps the enterprise integrate its many separately developed systems. It helps plan better systems and procedures, and link I.S. expenditures to top management goals. It helps remove bugs in system design. It helps to plan the hierarchy of critical success factors in an enterprise and to motivate managers to achieve what is critical. It helps to get the right information to the right people for effective control and decision making. The encyclopedia becomes an increasingly valuable corporate resource.

ARTIFICIAL INTELLIGENCE

In many organizations, well-planned databases have become a vital corporate asset. In the future, knowledge bases will be a vital asset. Expertise built into knowledgebases becomes steadily more refined, as it has in the Digital Equipment Corporation's pioneering use of expert systems. The existence of a maturing expert system affects everything that it touches. In DEC all salespeople will be expected to use an expert system (XSEL) for configuring, pricing, and controlling orders. Designers of new computers have a step in their procedures, which is the adding of knowledge needed for configuring the new systems to the configuration expert system (XCON). This computerized expert help must exist before the computer is announced. Details from the sales expert systems go to the factory expert systems, and delivery dates from the production planning expert system go to the salespeople. The production planning knowledgebase in turn affects other factory expert systems. The knowledge in such systems steadily accumulates, building up a computerized base of expertise for running the corporation as efficiently as possible. These expert systems use data that is in the corporate databases. Knowledge engineering should be an extension of information engineering.

The term *artificial intelligence* is used to encompass the building of expert systems. Artificial intelligence is a term which can be misleading because the computer cannot emulate human intelligence. The human brain is far more subtle than programs, and can recall and interlink a vast diversity of ideas. The techniques of artificial intelligence have given us *automated reasoning*. Using inference engine software, a computer can access facts and rules and chain together many rules to reach complex conclusions (without an application program). The facts and rules are garnered from human experts. The automated reasoning sometimes exceeds the reasoning ability of humans.

The early attempts to build expert systems have made several things clear [2]. First, there are vast numbers of potential applications of this technology. They surround us everywhere in business and government, if only management had the ability to recognize them. Second, the productivity which a knowledgeworker applies to a task often improves tenfold or more when automated reasoning is used. Third, most, but not all, expert systems can be built with and run on, personal computers. Fourth, automated reasoning needs to be used with existing databases, and should be an extension of database toolkits. Fifth, certain important classes of expert systems are easy to build. Sixth, the most advanced systems for automated reasoning far exceed human capability and give a major advance in our ability to build a computerized corporation.

Tom Peters, the coauthor of *In Search of Excellence,* wrote in his forward to the book *The Rise of the Expert Company* [3]:

> Any senior manager in any business of almost any size who isn't at least learning about AI, and sticking a tentative toe or two into AI's waters, is simply out of step, dangerously so.

The corporation of the future will make massive use of knowledgebases and automated reasoning. Expertise will be captured and accumulated. Every knowledge worker will use a workstation with access to computerized expertise, and as automation spreads almost *all* workers will become knowledge workers. Competitive success will, to a large extent, depend upon the quality of the human and computerized knowledge in the enterprise.

NETWORKS AND STANDARDS

Data communication is vital to the running of corporations. Just as there is a telephone on everyone's desk today, so there will be a workstation on everyone's desk in the future. The data network is the nervous system of the corporation; the workstations are its nerve endings.

The workstations give access to information. The capability to process this information, display it graphically, do computations with it, and make decisions with it, will often reside locally even though the data may have been extracted from databases far away. Often the workstation will be a personal computer; sometimes it will be a terminal of a departmental computer or system designed for a group of employees.

The workstation software and hardware will avoid the need to use coded commands and punctuation, which most people find difficult. It will replace any form of alien syntax with easy-to-learn, user-seductive forms of dialog employing techniques such as icons, graphics, a mouse, pull-down menus with deci-second response times, windows, scrolling, a screen desktop analogy, and natural human language. All employees in efficient corporations of the future will be expected to be able to use the workstations.

The databases to which these workstations have access will be designed to be flexible and to make it easy to extract information for local manipulation. The software connecting the workstation to the machines with databases will give transparent windows into these machines.

To achieve the connectability that is desired, network standards are extremely important. The desk workstation or departmental computer needs to access computers and databases anywhere in the organization in a transparent fashion. Network standards need to facilitate the transparent interconnection of machines from different vendors. Selecting and enforcing the network standards is a vital part of the strategic planning for networks in an organization. The standards apply to worldwide communications, communications satellites, local area networks, and any transmission media. Local area networks are important for obtaining fast response times, fast screen painting, and desk-to-desk communications within a building complex.

**BUILDING
HUMAN
POTENTIAL**

As computerized tools, robot machinery, and automated process control become more powerful, people tend to move into jobs of greater responsibility which require more skill. Often, they are more interesting jobs with higher pay. The annual revenue generated per person in highly automated corporations is often greater than $200,000 per person, whereas that in corporations with little automation is often less than $60,000 per person. The automated corporation demands greater skills for greater pay. In the Saturn plant of General Motors the mind-destroying job of the car production-line worker has been replaced with a more intelligent job for workers who carry out a set of tasks as the car moves through automated assembly stations. Human beings no longer act like robots on a relentlessly moving production line; robot-like work is *done* by robots. A new union contract has been negotiated for the new-style car workers which gives them a salary and profit sharing. In a similar way, moronic clerical work is tending to be replaced. Work with paper forms is disappearing. Bookkeepers are no longer adding up columns of figures. Financial staff, working with spreadsheets and decision-support tools, are expected to make more intelligent decisions. Loan officers, maintenance personnel, diagnostic technicians, and production schedulers will have access to expert systems. Systems analysts and programmers use more sophisticated tools giving them more power to be creative.

As technological potential is built up, so human potential must be built up with it. Efficient technological corporations such as IBM and DEC pay much attention to building human skills to keep pace with the growing demands and opportunities of technology. If a human being is left to do a moronic job for too long, the ability to upgrade his work skills becomes diminished. There has been a startling lack of success in attempts to retrain car production-line workers to do more interesting work. If you are 40 and have spent 20 years of your life on a car production line, you probably have a level of mental fossilization that makes it almost impossible for you to learn more demanding jobs.

The corporation with its eye on the future attempts to develop the skills of its employees so that they can succeed well with the technology that is coming. Secretaries use electronic mail and spreadsheets. Office workers are made computer literate. Blue-collar workers are introduced to more automated machines or operate multiple types of machine tools. Use of the most valuable types of personal computer software is encouraged. Managers should be involved in ISP and BAA studies. End users should be involved in IE/JAD sessions and should learn how to use the tools advocated by information centers. Experts of many types should take an interest in expert systems which might multiply their influence. All employees should be encouraged to think creatively about how the procedures they use can be improved.

THREE WAVES OF ENTRY IN TECHNOLOGY

Corporations tend to divide into three categories in their adoption of new technology. First there are the pioneers (Fig. 8.2). These are a small fraction of all corporations. The cost of pioneering may be high. The pioneers face substantial startup costs and the problems to be overcome in pioneering in order to gain a major competitive advantage through being first. American Airlines, for example, gained a major competitive advantage from having the world's first on-line seat reservation system, and then, years later, gained a still larger advantage by placing terminals in the offices of travel agents, connected to an expanded version of its system. Both of these pioneering systems were expensive high-risk developments that had a large payoff.

A second wave of corporations move into a technology when the pioneers

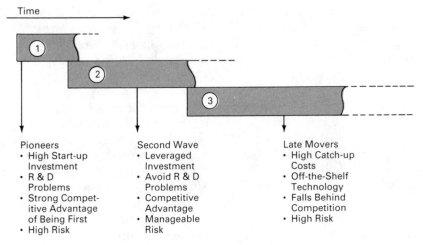

Pioneers
- High Start-up Investment
- R & D Problems
- Strong Competitive Advantage of Being First
- High Risk

Second Wave
- Leveraged Investment
- Avoid R & D Problems
- Competitive Advantage
- Manageable Risk

Late Movers
- High Catch-up Costs
- Off-the-Shelf Technology
- Falls Behind Competition
- High Risk

Figure 8.2

have demonstrated that it can be made to work. By this time there are lessons to be learned from the pioneer; there are seminars to attend; there are products on the market that have been tried, tested, and improved. There are far fewer research and development problems. The startup costs are lower. The risk is manageable. The first- and second-wave corporations are perhaps only 20 percent of all corporations, so there is still a strong competitive advantage to being second wave.

However, many corporations, production engineering departments, MIS departments, and so on, are set in their ways. They know how to manage their current technology and find many reasons for staying with it. Technicians, alarmed that they might become obsolete, find reasons for pouring scorn on the new ideas. The pioneers have already left to join another company. Many corporations and their technical departments avoid the need for upheaval until they are pushed into it. These late movers then have high catchup costs. They often do not have the technical staff they need. By the time they implement the new technology they have fallen severely behind their competition. Sometimes they never catch up with the early adapters but instead, buy services or move into less high-tech business areas. Being a late adapter to advanced technologies constitutes a high business risk.

Late adapters have the expense of conversion but do not gain competitive advantage from the conversion. They may have difficulty managing the conversion well, even though the technology is now off-the-shelf and stable. The last airlines to put in on-line reservation systems had the expense but no competitive advantage. The late adapters were not able to put terminals in travel agents' offices but had to buy services, often from their competition. The late adapters to factory automation with robots and CIM may not be able to manufacture goods cheaply enough to sell them against their competition. With some technological changes the late adapters will not stay in business.

GOVERNMENT

It is hoped that government departments of the future will be equally efficient in automation, but today, around the world, many public enterprises are not achieving the productivity through computers that is found in good private corporations. Government departments are usually immune from the intense competitive pressures that drive private corporations to automate. In industry there is a pressure to reduce headcount, to reduce costs, whereas in government, people-consuming bureaucracy tends to spread. In noncompetitive enterprises tangible goals need to be established (at the top of the pyramid) that replace the driving forces which stem from competition.

SUMMARY

It is difficult to see a revolution when one is in the middle of it. Today we are in the middle of a revolution concerning mankind's work. The social implications of this are great and I have discussed these elsewhere [4]. When the revolution is complete we will have highly automated factories, distribution channels, and services with highly integrated networks of computers. In the decade of the 1980s the total computer power delivered to U.S. industry, measured in instructions per second, increased 1000-fold. Much of this increase is from the spread of personal computers and departmental computers. These widely distributed computers will become much more powerful and will need to be integrated with each other and with mainframes. The corporation of the future will be run with a vast mesh of interacting computers and data-based systems. It will be impossible to manage and build the procedures to take advantage of this technology without some form of information engineering, appropriately automated. The encyclopedia, which is the heart of information engineering, will be a vital corporate resource.

Historians of the future will look back at the evolution of computing, destined to change so much in society, and will be amazed that the early attempts at data processing were done by hand. They will marvel that corporations survived the early incompatible spaghetti-mess that computing was before information engineering.

REFERENCES

1. Peter F. Drucker, "Playing in the Information-Based 'Orchestra,'" *The Wall Street Journal*, June 4, 1985.

2. *Artificial Intelligence, Applications and Design*, a videotape course of 8 tapes from Advanced Learning Inc., Naperville, IL, 1988.

3. E. Feigenbaum, P. McCorduck, H. P. Nii, *The Rise of the Expert Company*, Times Books, New York, 1988.

4. James Martin, *Technology's Crucible*, Prentice-Hall, Inc., Englewood Cliffs, NJ, 1986.

INDEX

TEAR OUT THIS PAGE TO ORDER OTHER TITLES BY JAMES MARTIN

THE JAMES MARTIN BOOKS

Quantity	Title	Title Code	Price	Total $
_____	Action Diagrams: Clearly Structured Specifications, Programs, and Procedures, 2nd Edition	00426–7	$20.00	_____
_____	Application Development Without Programmers	03894–3	$63.00	_____
_____	A Breakthrough In Making Computers Friendly: The Macintosh Computer (paper)	08157–0	$26.95	_____
_____	(case)	08158–8	$37.00	_____
_____	Building Expert Systems: A Tutorial	08624–9	$50.00	_____
_____	Communications Satellite Systems	15316–3	$69.00	_____
_____	Computer Data-Base Organization, 2nd Edition	16542–3	$65.00	_____
_____	The Computerized Society	16597–7	$32.00	_____
_____	Computer Networks and Distributed Processing: Software, Techniques and Architecture	16525–8	$63.00	_____
_____	Data Communication Technology	19664–2	$51.00	_____
_____	DB2: Concepts, Design, and Programming	19858–0	$48.00	_____
_____	Design and Strategy of Distributed Data Processing	20165–7	$67.00	_____
_____	Design of Man-Computer Dialogues	20125–1	$65.00	_____
_____	Design of Real-Time Computer Systems	20140–0	$65.00	_____
_____	Diagramming Techniques for Analysts and Programmers	20879–3	$59.00	_____
_____	An End User's Guide to Data Base	27712–9	$49.00	_____
_____	Fourth-Generation Languages, Vol. I: Principles	32967–2	$49.00	_____
_____	Fourth-Generation Languages, Vol. II: Representative 4GLs	32974–8	$48.00	_____
_____	Fourth-Generation Languages, Vol. III: 4GLs from IBM	32976–3	$48.00	_____
_____	Future Developments in Telecommunications, 2nd Edition	34585–0	$64.00	_____
_____	An Information Systems Manifesto	46476–8	$58.00	_____
_____	Introduction to Teleprocessing	49981–4	$53.00	_____
_____	Local Area Networks: Architectures and Implementations	53964–3	$40.00	_____
_____	Managing the Data-Base Environment	55058–2	$65.00	_____
_____	Principles of Data-Base Management	70891–7	$51.00	_____
_____	Principles of Data Communication	70989–9	$46.00	_____
_____	Recommended Diagramming Standards for Analysts and Programmers	76737–6	$53.00	_____
_____	Security, Accuracy, and Privacy in Computer Systems	79899–1	$65.00	_____
_____	SNA: IBM's Networking Solution	81514–2	$50.00	_____
_____	Software Maintenance: The Problem and Its Solutions	82236–1	$58.00	_____
_____	Strategic Data Planning Methodologies	85111–3	$51.00	_____
_____	Structured Techniques: The Basis for CASE, Revised Edition	85493–5	$57.00	_____
_____	Systems Analysis for Data Transmission	88130–0	$67.00	_____
_____	System Design from Provably Correct Constructs	88148–2	$58.00	_____

(over)

_____	Technology's Crucible (paper)	90202-3	$15.95 _____
_____	Telecommunications and the Computer, 2nd Edition	90249-4	$62.00 _____
_____	Telematic Society: A Challenge for Tomorrow	90246-0	$31.95 _____
_____	Teleprocessing Network Organization	90245-2	$40.00 _____
_____	VSAM: Access Method Services and Programming Techniques	94417-3	$50.00 _____

Total:_____

-discount (if appropriate)_____

New Total:_____

AND TAKE ADVANTAGE OF THESE SPECIAL OFFERS!

When ordering 3 or 4 copies (of the same or different titles) take 10% off the total list price.

When ordering 5 to 20 (of the same or different titles) take 15% off the total list price.

To receive a greater discount when ordering more than 20 copies, call or write:

Special Sales Department
College Marketing
Prentice Hall
Englewood Cliffs, NJ 07632
(201)592-2046

SAVE!

If payment accompanies order, plus your state's sales tax where applicable, Prentice Hall pays postage and handling charges. Same return privilege refund guarantee. Please do not mail cash.

☐ **PAYMENT ENCLOSED**—shipping and handling to be paid by publisher (please include your state's tax where applicable)

☐ **SEND BOOKS ON 15-DAY TRIAL BASIS** and bill me (with small charge for shipping and handling).

Name _____

Address _____

City _____ State _____ Zip _____
I prefer to charge my   ☐ Visa   ☐ MasterCard

Card Number _____ Expiration Date _____

Signature _____

All prices listed are subject to change without notice.
This offer not valid outside U.S.

Mail your order to: Prentice Hall Book Distribution Center
Route 59 at Brook Hill Drive
West Nyack, NY 10994

Dept. 1 D-JMAR-NK(4)

Information Systems Management and Strategy	Methodologies for Building Systems	Analysis and Design	CASE
AN INFORMATION SYSTEMS MANIFESTO	STRATEGIC INFORMATION PLANNING METHODOLOGIES (second edition)	STRUCTURED TECHNIQUES: THE BASIS FOR CASE (revised edition)	STRUCTURED TECHI THE BASIS FOR C (revised edition
INFORMATION ENGINEERING (Volume I: Introduction and Principles)	INFORMATION ENGINEERING (Volume I: Introduction and Principles)	DATABASE ANALYSIS AND DESIGN	DIAGRAMMING STAI FOR CASE
INFORMATION ENGINEERING (Volume II: Strategy and Analysis)	INFORMATION ENGINEERING (Volume II: Strategy and Analysis)	DESIGN OF MAN-COMPUTER DIALOGUES	INFORMATION ENGIN (Volume I: Introdu and Principles)
STRATEGIC INFORMATION PLANNING METHODOLOGIES (second edition)	INFORMATION ENGINEERING (Volume III: Design and Construction)	DESIGN OF REAL-TIME COMPUTER SYSTEMS	**Languages and Progr**
SOFTWARE MAINTENANCE: THE PROBLEM AND ITS SOLUTIONS	STRUCTURED TECHNIQUES: THE BASIS FOR CASE (revised edition)	DATA COMMUNICATIONS DESIGN TECHNIQUES	APPLICATION DEVELO WITHOUT PROGRAM
DESIGN AND STRATEGY FOR DISTRIBUTED DATA PROCESSING	**Diagramming Techniques**	DESIGN AND STRATEGY FOR DISTRIBUTED DATA PROCESSING	FOURTH-GENERAT LANGUAGES (Volume I: Princip
CORPORATE COMMUNICATIONS STRATEGY	DIAGRAMMING TECHNIQUES FOR ANALYSTS AND PROGRAMMERS	SOFTWARE MAINTENANCE: THE PROBLEM AND ITS SOLUTIONS	FOURTH-GENERAT LANGUAGES (Volume II: Representativ
Expert Systems	RECOMMENDED DIAGRAMMING STANDARDS FOR ANALYSTS AND PROGRAMMERS	SYSTEM DESIGN FROM PROVABLY CORRECT CONSTRUCTS	FOURTH-GENERAT LANGUAGES (Volume III: 4GLs from
BUILDING EXPERT SYSTEMS: A TUTORIAL	DIAGRAMMING STANDARDS FOR CASE	INFORMATION ENGINEERING (Volume II: Strategy and Analysis)	ACTION DIAGRAMS: C STRUCTURED SPECIFIC PROGRAMS, AND PROC (second edition)
KNOWLEDGE ACQUISITION FOR EXPERT SYSTEMS	ACTION DIAGRAMS: CLEARLY STRUCTURED SPECIFICATIONS, PROGRAMS, AND PROCEDURES (second edition)	INFORMATION ENGINEERING (Volume III: Design and Construction)	
		SAA: IBM's SYSTEMS APPLICATION ARCHITECTURE	